Invisible Nation

Invisible Nation

Homeless Families in America

Richard Schweid

UNIVERSITY OF CALIFORNIA PRESS

University of California Press, one of the most distin-
guished university presses in the United States, enriches
lives around the world by advancing scholarship in the
humanities, social sciences, and natural sciences. Its
activities are supported by the UC Press Foundation and
by philanthropic contributions from individuals and
institutions. For more information, visit www.ucpress.edu.

University of California Press
Oakland, California

A small portion of Chapter 1 appeared in *Oxford American*,
Spring 2008.

Library of Congress Cataloging-in-Publication Data

Names: Schweid, Richard, 1946- author.
Title: Invisible nation : homeless families in America /
Richard Schweid.
Description: Oakland, California : University of
California Press, [2016] | Includes bibliographical
references and index.
Identifiers: LCCN 2016009774 | ISBN 9780520292666 (cloth :
alk. paper) | ISBN 9780520292673 (pbk. : alk. paper) |
ISBN 9780520966093 (ebook)
Subjects: LCSH: Homelessness—United States—Case
studies. | Poverty—United States—Case studies.
Classification: LCC HV4505 .S39 2016 | DDC 362.5/920973—dc23
LC record available at http://lccn.loc.gov/2016009774

Manufactured in the United States of America

25 24 23 22 21 20 19 18 17 16
10 9 8 7 6 5 4 3 2 1

For Daniel Winunwe Rivers, Jessica Delgado,
and Kaya Delgado Rivers

There is nothing new about poverty. What is new is that we now have the techniques and the resources to get rid of poverty. The real question is whether we have the will.

—Martin Luther King, Jr., preaching in Washington, DC's, National Cathedral on March 31, 1968, five days before he was assassinated.

CONTENTS

The Family Room

A place to sleep. For most of us, it is a given in our lives, along with a roof over our heads and our own front door to close. But ever since the beginnings of the European colonization of North America—Jamestown in 1607, and the *Mayflower* pilgrims' Plymouth Colony in 1620—communities on these shores have had to deal with those among them who did *not* have a place to sleep, people who could not provide for themselves or their children and had no one to give them shelter.

Despite the fact that the New World offered any able-bodied person an abundance of game, seafood, and fertile soil, life was not easy. Disease, war, and accident were constantly thinning the ranks of the colonists, leaving their families to fend for themselves. A woman could be widowed in the blink of an eye, the loosing of an arrow, or the bite of a mosquito. Widows and children who had depended on a man's hard work could suddenly be left with no support. Women bled to death during childbirth or were cut down by fevers, leaving a man behind to raise the children. For one reason or another some people have always found themselves trying to maintain families in the most precarious of conditions.

From the Plymouth Colony until today, public officials have generally, if reluctantly, accepted the idea that they were responsible for the care of the desperately poor among them. Local governments to some degree have always accepted an obligation to care for the poor, particularly indigent families with children.

In the winter of 2002 I was staying at a Dearborn, Michigan, motel, researching a completely different topic, when I began to wonder how that obligation was currently being met. Each morning I would rise in my room and go down the hallway to the lobby for free donuts and coffee. Each morning four small, neatly dressed and groomed kids—two boys, two girls—were standing by the front door waiting for a school bus, peering out, packs on their backs.

One morning curiosity moved me to ask the desk clerk who they were. "Homeless," he answered. "The county sent them."

Their families must have had an unusually nasty run of bad luck, I ventured. No, he said, the local shelter for homeless families was full, and the motel—on the outer reaches of Michigan Avenue—was always home to some of the overflow population, rooms paid for at $60 a night by Wayne County. One room to a family. Then he added, "But don't worry. We don't let the kids have any donuts in the morning. Those are only for our paying guests."

In the afternoons the kids ran up and down the hall or kicked a ball from one end to the other. The raw Michigan winter made it too cold to play outside for any length of time, and they had energy to burn. It was hard for me to believe that children in the United States were being raised in motel rooms with nowhere else to play but long, narrow hallways on dirty, threadbare carpeting. I began to read about homeless families.

While the question of how to relieve families living in desperate poverty has a long history, the present situation is different and perhaps worse than it has ever been. Never before has the number of homeless included so many single women with children. Fifty years ago the word "homeless" signified dysfunctional individuals—mostly men—who drank heavily and slept rough. Now it is more likely to mean a young single mother with small children and a minimum-wage job. In 1980 families with children made up only 1 percent of the nation's homeless; by 2014 that number was 37 percent of the total.[1]

Naïvely, I was shocked to learn that over the course of 2002 more than a million children were homeless in the richest nation in the world. They were living in motel rooms, in cars, in shelters, or doubled and tripled up, packed into the houses of family or friends, the only constant condition being too many people in too little space. An estimated one in every ten of these homeless children lived in a motel, and their families usually included a single parent who could not get enough rent and deposit together at the same time for an apartment, but who was able to scrape by week to week paying for a room. Many of these single parents held minimum-wage jobs. A whole family would live in that room—brothers, sisters, and usually just a mother, though occasionally a man was around too. Furnishings included a microwave, two double beds, a bureau, and a big motel television.

Over the years that have passed since I was in Dearborn, the number of homeless families in the United States has skyrocketed. In 2006 up to 1.6 million children were homeless at some time during the year, and by 2014 the number had risen to 2.5 million.[2] In 2013 twenty million people were living in deep poverty with incomes less than half of the official poverty rate; this was almost three times the number who were in such desperate straits in 1976.[3]

The growing gap between the haves and the have-nots has created a huge pool of extremely poor families unmatched since the Great Depression, a vast floodtide of people adrift with nothing to hold on to. They spend long days and nights just getting by, trying to make it through another week without spending money on anything but food and shelter while putting off going to the dentist, or the doctor, or getting the car repaired. Although they are frequently without resources, they must deal with the same problems as the rest of us: illness, debt, substance abuse, sons and daughters in trouble, and the other misfortunes that nip at our heels as we try to get through our days.

This kind of deep family poverty is happening not in isolated pockets across the country but in cities, counties, and states from one end of the nation to the other. Somewhere in our home state, in every state, children are growing up in motel rooms; others are living in cars. That they are below our communal radar is generally okay with their parents: to draw attention can bring trouble. These are not mentally ill people walking the streets wrapped in blankets, or chronically homeless individuals pushing supermarket carts full of all they own. These are mothers trying to keep their children fed, sheltered, and out of the hands of the authorities.

We are apt not to notice them. Life goes on and most of us have all we can do to make it to the other side of any given twenty-four hours without taking note of the homeless families around us. We go through our daily lives with little or no awareness of the rising tide of unanchored, struggling people who are about to go under at any moment and bring their children down with them. A terrible drama is playing out, perhaps only a few blocks from where we are living our own complicated, relatively comfortable lives.

It may seem that these people's plights do not directly affect us. Nevertheless, when so many live among us in such hardship, their presence inevitably will have consequences for our communities, eroding the underpinnings of the very society that nurtures us and forms our world. What does it mean if we are thriving when so many people around us are living in misery and having such a hard time getting through each day? What does it mean for them, and what does it mean for us?

It turns out that the question of how to relieve the poorest among us has bedeviled public officials and policy makers for centuries. The biblical declaration that the poor will always be with us has held true throughout our nation's history. Over the centuries only a limited number of options have been found to deal with these families: some type of direct material support to keep them housed and fed; institutionalization in an almshouse or shelter; or placing the children somewhere outside the biological family, either in another home or in an institutional setting such as an orphanage. Variations of each of these solutions have been employed since the first white colonists reached America, and they continue to be applied today, five centuries later, with varying degrees of success.

Two basic schools of thought have always existed. Today these schools often are referred to by social scientists as "structural" and "individual." The former holds that the root cause of a family's extreme poverty is likely to rest with social context: little or no available employment; a lack of education; a dysfunctional family; no access to social services; an exorbitantly high rental market.

The second school assigns the blame for a family's desperate circumstances to some personal failure by the head of the family, some vice or weakness of character, an inability to get along in the world that is a person's own fault but for which the family must bear the burden. Poverty is the price to be paid for a life frittered away in substance abuse, promiscuity, or laziness.

In 1897 no less a figure than a past director of the United States Census, Francis Walker, wrote: "Pauperism is, in truth, largely voluntary, to the full degree in which anything can be said to be voluntary in a world of causation—a matter, if not of definite and conscious choice, then of appetites and aptitudes indulged or submitted to from inherent baseness or cowardice or moral weakness. Those who are paupers are so far more from character than from condition. They have the pauper taint; they bear the pauper brand."[4]

Today as ever, opinions about poverty are closely linked to political affiliation and class. A 2014 poll found that nearly 60 percent of Republicans believe poverty is the result of decisions individuals have taken, compared with only 24 percent of Democrats.[5] The belief that the poor are primarily responsible for their own plights mitigates, if not annuls, the public responsibility to provide decent room and board to those who cannot provide it for themselves. A substantial segment of our society still holds that to provide more than the barest of assistance to homeless families is to encourage them in shiftlessness and discourage them from bettering themselves.

As politicians, bureaucrats, social service workers, and policy makers spend years, even decades, debating whether and how to help these families, the homeless children in them grow up to adulthood and are incorporated into society. They move among us, many of them scarred, scared, and emotionally stunted for life, growing into parents who will raise yet another generation of extremely poor children. Some few of these children, through hard work, focus, and good luck, will grow up to pull themselves out of poverty, but most will never have an opportunity to do so. Various studies are commissioned; ten-year plans are elaborated to end family homelessness; municipal committees are formed to implement the plans. All the while, the gap continues to grow between rich and poor, with more and more people sliding toward the bottom, taking their families with them.

I for one did not have any idea that so many children were adrift around me, and the more miles I logged traveling within this invisible nation, the more I was astonished by their numbers. What also became clear as I spoke with homeless parents, interviewed social service providers, and read histories of family poverty in the United States was that today we have the capacity to eradicate this twenty-first-century plague of family homelessness; we know how to do it; we need only commit to doing so. Hopefully, the following report about the past, present, and future of the invisible nation will encourage that commitment.

CHAPTER ONE

Nashville, Tennessee

Off the Charts in Music City

> Those who are poor and in infancy or childhood ...
> have a right to require from society a distinct attention
> and more scrupulous and precise supervision. Their
> career of existence has but just commenced. They may
> be rendered blessings or scourges to society. Their
> course may be happy or miserable, honorable or
> disgraceful, according to the specific nature of the
> provision made for their support and education.
>
> From an 1821 Massachusetts legislative
> committee report authored by Josiah Quincy[1]

I grew up in Nashville and now figured it would serve me as well as any other place to appreciate the realities faced by homeless families. My childhood there was housed and privileged in a prosperous suburb. Setting out on this project, I knew I might gain no real insight into the daily lives of homeless families by living briefly side by side with them. These were people who were trapped and sinking, while I had the ultimate privilege of being able to leave whenever I wanted. To think I could parachute into their lives and understand anything much in a few weeks was a gross presumption. No one willingly jumps into homelessness; people fall into it. It's a pit. But at least I would be breathing the same air as they were, seeing the same sights in front of my eyes, suffering for a moment in the same sinkhole. I wanted to understand how this could be happening in the United States, what was done over the past centuries to deal with family homelessness, and what is—or is not—being done today.

Single men are not allowed in family shelters, so those doors were closed to me. While the majority of homeless families live doubled or tripled up with family and friends, I reasoned they would be hard pressed to find room for me in their lives. I could however pay for a motel room and live among that sizeable minority of homeless families who find themselves doing the same.

I started my research in November 2003, at the Trinity Inn motel. The tools I brought to the job were few and easily assembled: glasses, rental car keys, Swiss Army knife, wallet, reporter's notebook, ballpoint pen, and a handheld tape recorder, a $39.95 analog item, the only specialized tool required. A dulled sense of shock and outrage also helped. I would be spending time in the neighborhood around the motel, putting my nose into other people's business, asking questions, recording interviews, trying to get an idea of what life was like for the millions of children who were living in motel rooms across the United States for a few weeks, or months, or years of their lives.

The Trinity Inn was close to an exit off Interstate 65 south. It was alongside four-lane Dickerson Pike, a five-minute drive from downtown Nashville in a neighborhood given over to folks having a rough go of it, people who were living in motels and trailer parks. It was a neighborhood that repeated itself in all of the nation's midsized and small cities: convenience stores doing a big business in cigarettes, beer, and lottery tickets; used-car lots with prices soaped on the front windshields of vehicles on offer; check-cashing storefronts; and chain discount stores offering cheap goods to poor people with uncertain futures. The occasional sign in Spanish—"El Mecanico" chalked on a big blackboard in front of a rickety garage with a tin roof— indicated the presence of a certain Latino population, but the vast majority of Dickerson Pike's residents were poor black or white Nashvillians.

"This was a middle-class neighborhood in the Fifties," long-time resident Michael Douglas told me. He was balding, white, fifty years old, and the owner of Charlie Bob's Restaurant, a meat-and-three-sides place, the only real eatery remaining on the Pike and a good one. He was also its cook. "Dickerson Pike was a major route in and out of Nashville. My dad bought two motels here. They were both rated Triple A by the Automobile Association. That was the best rating they gave. This was before 1968 when the interstate went in. It killed everything. When things began to go downhill, my dad sold the motels. People bought them for the girls working the street to use."

Use them they did, and use them they still do. Sex industry workers were not in short supply along Dickerson Pike. Women wearing far too few clothes for the weather, all dressed up with no apparent place to go, could be found walking along the sides of the Pike at almost any hour. As I was leaving the motel one evening, a young woman with long, stringy, blonde hair and a spotty complexion was standing in an open doorway of a room a few doors from mine. She met my eye as I pulled hard on the door behind me checking to make sure it had locked. She asked for a ride down the road to the Dickerson Pike market, a convenience store a few blocks away. It was cold and drizzling and she had on a thin, blue shiny satin jacket.

"I'm Red," she introduced herself when she was settled in the front seat, although the reddest thing about her was her left eye, bloodshot and drooping. "You get high?"

"No. I used to," I said companionably.

"Well, I don't know what you're doing here, then. Everybody at this place gets high. You date?"

"No, I've got a girlfriend."

I dropped her off at the market and when I drove back by half an hour later she was still there, standing under an edge of the store roof's overhang, thin jacket slick and gleaming under an outside light in the cold, wet night air. I almost stopped to offer her a ride, but didn't, and drove on back to the motel. My room was a world in itself although not one in which you'd want to raise your children. It had an emerald-green carpet pocked with brown cigarette burns that looked like cockroaches in the dim light of the one overhead bulb—and sometimes they were.

The drawers in the room's scarred bureau were so nasty that I left my underclothes in my suitcase and took care to keep it shut. An oppressively heavy smell of old cigarette smoke hung in the air; it had seeped into the walls, mirror, and every surface. The room had no wastebasket. Neither did the tiny bathroom, with its mildewed shower curtain, rust-streaked tub and sink. I hung a plastic bag from a nail in the wall for my trash. No cups or glasses were provided. In return for my $150 a week, someone dumped off a napless towel and a change of bedding each Friday, and the gray sheets always had a few small holes in them.

One night about 11 P.M., half asleep, propped up on the wide bed watching the big television on top of the bureau, I was jerked to wakefulness by a banging on my door. I opened it to a guy about my size, short and skinny, with Latino features. His dark brown eyes were out of control, flashing with need. He looked like some fierce little beast inside him was struggling to get out. "Gimme some," he growled.

"I'm not whoever you think I am, and I don't have anything to give you."

"Man, gimme some," he hissed, rearing back, desperate with urgency.

"I don't have anything," I repeated, shutting the door hard and waiting, breath held, to see if he would knock again. He didn't.

The front desk at the Trinity Inn was a thick plastic shield with a round hole in it through which the public could speak to a motel employee should one happen to be there, which was not likely. Taped up beside the hole was a printed list of a dozen "Rules for Guests." Some, such as the one reading "No visitors after 9 P.M.," were not taken seriously. People came and went all night; knocks rang out on doors; voices rose and fell; cars idled in the parking lot under the shadowy lighting, plumes of smoke issuing out of their tailpipes into the cold air. Or the rule "All visitors must sign in at the office." I never saw anyone doing so. Most of the time no one was in the office. To speak with motel staff it was easier to knock on the door of the room behind the office, or go across the parking lot to the convenience store. One posted rule taken seriously at the Trinity Inn read "Anyone evicted will have their things thrown away."

On a regular basis families were evicted from rooms for not paying the rent; they were locked out and all their belongings inside were forfeited. Children's toys and favorite things were gone forever. Anyone who has ever watched a young child form an attachment to some beat-up raggedy doll, some scrap of material, or the way children pour all of themselves, their affection, anger, everything into one object and who with nothing more than that scrap can sleep soundly just about anywhere, will understand that its sudden overnight loss may generate terrible anxiety. Kids regularly arrived at school with only the shirts on their backs. Textbooks needed to be replaced.

It happened frequently enough that teachers at Shwab Elementary School, with 350 students from kindergarten through fourth grade, kept sets of kids' clothes in various sizes laundered and tucked away in drawers. The school sat almost directly across the four lanes of Dickerson Pike from the Trinity Inn. It was a solid and safe two-story brick building, opened in 1890, permanent and anchored, built back behind a grassy turnaround that set the school well off the Pike. Inside it was a school like any school, providing a structured day with rules to follow and things to learn. In 2003 about 75 percent of the Shwab Elementary student body had been homeless at some point in their young lives. Many of the kids who began the academic year enrolled at Shwab in September would be attending a different school by the end of the year in June. Some had changed schools more than a dozen times by the end of second grade.

Life for the children who lived in a half dozen motels scattered around Dickerson Pike—each of which usually had some homeless families among its tenants—was a long way from the childhood most Nashvillians had. This was a part of town in which I had never found myself in more than thirty years of living in Nashville as a child and an adult. Most who did pass this way drove through with their car doors locked. There were no community centers around the Pike, nor libraries, and because of the neighborhood's dubious character even the Bookmobile would not serve it. "The closest libraries are a couple of bus stops away," said Paula Poag, a reading teacher at Shwab. "People who don't have the money to pay their rent are not going to be spending bus fare to go to the library. Kids here have nothing.[2]

"These families living in motel rooms, cooking on hot plates, might be a mom, dad, and two or three kids in one room. They might have a pet. The kids don't go home to anything close to a quiet, calm environment. Everything's in upheaval, even if they're not moving. And, they move a lot. Our turnover is always greatest on the day the rent is due. That's when people move around.

"It's a huge problem," said Poag, with a grimace. She was a young, round-faced, blonde woman with a certain air of tenderness, who seemed like she would be a fine teacher. Our interview in the "reading room" was regularly interrupted by kids coming in with a note that needed signing or a question that needed answering. She gave them all the same firm response: "Miss Poag is in a meeting now, dear," and sent them on to another room.

"I think Shwab has the highest number of homeless students in Nashville," she told me. "We are considered the prime school that the Homeless Act affects." The Homeless Act, otherwise known as the McKinney Homeless Assistance Act, was passed into federal law in 1987 and later rebaptized the McKinney-Vento Act. It mandates that each public school and public school system provide a certain set of services for children who are homeless. One of the most effective things it did was to define which students in fact should be considered homeless. Since its passage the number of children falling under its provisions has grown steadily.

"It involves people living in hotels, motels, weekly rentals, and trailer parks, as well as in shelters and doubled up with relatives," explained Poag. "Our trailer parks are our most stable population. Those are the people who stay. We have people in some of the trailer parks who have lived there for generations, almost like a lot of public housing. Grandmother lives there, then everyone moves on in. That's kind of what our trailer parks are like. It's more of a generational thing."

Not if they were in the kind of trailer that Jennifer Page* rented, in which she and her three kids lived at the back of a Dickerson Pike mobile home park a few blocks north of Shwab School. Her trailer did not look like it had a generation's worth of use left in it. The front of the park was ordered with neat spaces, well-kept mobile homes one next to the other, each with a little rectangle of grassy ground, the miniature yards shaded by tall, old trees—oaks, hickories, and walnuts. It was indeed possible to imagine generations living in them. But the one road into the place continued back behind the bulk of the park, down a dip where a creek ran through a culvert under the pavement, and up a rise; on one side undergrowth and brambly blackberry bushes, on the other run-down trailers. A half dozen small cats lolled in the sun on the road, ambling aside when a car passed.

Jennifer Page and her two youngest children—a brother and sister, five and three years old—slept in one bedroom, and her oldest son, twelve, had another smaller, closet-sized room. Mildew seemed well advanced in the ceiling of his room; the small bathroom smelled rank; a ragged hole had been punched into its particle-board wall. The back bedroom was almost entirely filled by the mattress for three and a small table with a television on it. Another wider TV sat at one end of the living room, across from a broken-down couch covered with a paisley-print cloth.

At thirty-nine Jennifer Page had done some hard living and it showed in her face. She had deep, dark circles under her eyes. Still it was not hard to imagine she was once a lovely young woman—she also had long blonde hair, bright blue eyes, and a

---

* An asterisk denotes people whose names have been changed.

quick smile. She had red polish on her fingernails, but her hands were rough; the skin of her fingers was cracked. She did not blame what had happened in her life on anyone or anything other than herself and bad luck, she told me. Like me she had been raised in another part of the city, in what she said was a standard Nashville middle-class household.

"My parents were pretty well-off and we had it made. We weren't wealthy, but we had a nice home and two cars, and my parents worked. Then they got divorced and things just kind of fell apart from there. I've got no family left, really. My father passed away three years ago. I have one brother and he's in the federal penitentiary in Arizona. So, it's just me, nobody to turn to. I've had a hard row to hoe."[3]

She did not graduate from high school and had held a number of minimum-wage jobs: telemarketer, waitress, cashier. She left an abusive husband who gave her four children. Despite the run-down condition of the trailer, Page was glad to have been in it for the past six months. It was, she said, the third time she had lived in this trailer park, and this time she had arrived after living eleven months in the Colonial Inn, a motel a few blocks away.

Tears came into her eyes. "It's not what I want for my children. I want better for my kids. I see men and women every day struggling like me. There's people in this trailer park right now I could take you to who have nothing, zero; they live from day to day wondering where they're going to get their next meal, how they're going to pay their bills. It's not easy."

Her life had taken a sharp downward turn a couple of years before I met her, she told me, when her oldest son died of cerebral palsy. "I lost my job, and my son died, and I fell into substance abuse. I was taking pain pills. Dilaudid. Everything caught up with me. I was staying in another trailer park at the time, but I lost that place and we stayed for a week in my car. Three kids in that car," she nodded toward the front door of the trailer and the battered 1989 Honda parked outside.

"Then, I managed to get enough together for a week's rent at the motel. Week after week. It was so *hard* living there. I hope I never have to go through that again. But there's plenty of people that do. I was really surprised to see how many families were living at these motels around here. I don't know how they can do it. My kids stayed sick all the time cooped up in that room. The carpets were so nasty, and it was full of germs in there. I didn't understand why they were staying so sick and the doctor told me, 'It's that room you're in.'

"They never got any sunlight in there. I kept the curtains drawn all the time. I didn't want my kids seeing out and I didn't want nobody seeing in. It was horrible, horrible. I had to wash my dishes in the bathtub. A friend of mine gave me a little refrigerator and that's where I'd keep a half gallon of milk, maybe some lunch meat and cheese. I couldn't pay the extra they wanted for a microwave. We did a lot of eating of sandwiches. That's how we lived," she said, quietly.

"I was working at a fast-food restaurant and the kids got home before I did. I told them never to open the door. I had a key, so if someone knocked it wouldn't be me, and I told them if anyone ever did knock to be very quiet, not to make a sound. That's how we had to live. There were a lot of drugs, a lot of prostitution there. And killings, too, there was a lot of death up there. The kids had a bad time with it. It was scary. They started having nightmares."

Her oldest son, whose name was Joseph Charles*, was called J.C. He was a big kid, tall, and somewhat overweight. He had lively, kind brown eyes and was generally studious, his mother said. Before the family moved to the motel, he had been on the honor roll. "While we were staying at the motel, he would do his homework at night. It wasn't easy. All of us in one room, the TV would be on, the little ones would be playing. It all really got on the kids' nerves. [J.C.'s] grades started falling. My five-year-old got to the point where he was pulling his hair out, and the doctor said it was a nervous disorder."

The experience of Jennifer Page's family in their motel room was typical of what millions of families have lived through. A report issued by the National Center on Family Homelessness concluded that children who are homeless are in fair or poor health twice as often as other children and four times as often as children whose parents earn more than $35,000 a year. The report also noted that homeless children are more anxious and do less well in school, displaying a wide range of developmental problems.[4]

Growing up in a motel room does not necessarily limit a child's future to the lowest level of the socio-economic scale. It is possible to climb out of deep poverty even from a childhood involving homelessness, but it is much more difficult. Studies of homeless children repeatedly arrive at the same conclusion. Not surprisingly it is identical to the conclusion Page reached during her eleven months at the Colonial Inn: homelessness is not good for children. It puts them at increased risk for physical and behavioral problems.

A disproportionate number of homeless preschoolers have chronic illnesses. The most common are ear infections, asthma, stammering, and eczema. They are four times as likely to be asthmatic as other children.[5] Studies have concluded that there is no category of diseases to which only homeless children are vulnerable but that they are at significantly greater risk of suffering from numerous illnesses than the general pediatric population. Many of these health risks are associated more with

poverty than with homelessness. They are present for desperately poor housed children as well. But throwing homelessness
into the mix increases the potential for physical stress and psychological damage.

Many of these kids have already had more trauma in their
lives than is good for them. They are at greater risk of experiencing physical or sexual abuse. If they do not personally experience
it, they are more likely to witness violent incidents between adult
family members, often men physically abusing women. A safe,
secure world in which to learn and develop does not exist for
children exposed early and often to violence, whether that is
gunfire in the streets of their neighborhood, or a father beating a
mother, or someone beating them. The effects of such early
exposure are profound. Studies suggest that such experiences
not only contribute to mental illness in adults but also generate it
and can directly cause a range of mental problems including
chronic depression, impaired functioning, substance abuse disorders, and post-traumatic stress disorder (PTSD).[6]

Ellen Bassuk, a retired associate professor of psychiatry at Harvard Medical School and a founder and longtime president of the
National Center on Family Homelessness (NCFH), concluded
that the lifetime prevalence of these disorders was higher among
homeless mothers than among mothers with stable housing. Her
study compared 220 homeless families in Worcester, Massachusetts, to a control group of 216 low-income families that were
housed. Nearly a third of the homeless mothers she interviewed
had made at least one suicide attempt. She also found a significantly higher number of homeless mothers who were hospitalized
for emotional problems or substance abuse than housed mothers.[7]

"The average age of mothers heading up homeless families is
about twenty-seven years old," Bassuk told me in 2009. "Our

data show that 42 percent of them have been molested by the age of twelve, usually by multiple perpetrators. If you extrapolate that to a public school class, one out of every two kids there is being abused, and it probably is that high. Our society is very violent."[8]

She was a professor of psychiatry at Harvard when I first spoke with her, although she had little time to dedicate to academic pursuits. She was too busy as president of the NCFH. The center served as the oversight agency for government grants to "demonstration projects" at homeless service agencies around the country. It provided technical services, evaluated the projects, set up conferences, and worked with about forty different sites. She spent a lot of time traveling, including trips to Washington to testify before Congress when the issue of homeless families came up, which it did far too infrequently to suit her. She had spent three decades watching the problem worsen while public responses—way too little, way too late—failed to stem the growing numbers of homeless women and children.

Bassuk stepped down as president of the center in 2012, after serving as its director since its beginning in 1988, and she founded a new organization, the Center for Social Innovation. She had not set out to spend her professional life as an institutional advocate for homeless families. "I'm a doctor, I'm a medical doctor. I was on staff at one of the teaching hospitals in the early eighties. We started seeing an influx of individual homeless people with mental illness and we had no place to send them. I was asked to run a task force for then-governor Dukakis.

"I didn't know much about it, but I went into the shelters and I began to write about it, and I became the instant expert. In this country you write one article and you're it. They make you an expert and then you're in trouble," she laughed ruefully. By the end of the 1980s Bassuk's studies were increasingly alarming. She founded the NCFH and began to work with homeless families. The more she learned, the more she became convinced that simply looking at homelessness as a housing problem was wrong. It was also a health problem, often a mental health problem, frequently rooted in the violence that mothers and children routinely experienced.

"The hidden picture, the subtext of homelessness is violence," she told me when we spoke in 2009. "In this country, violence is completely enmeshed in the entire problem of homeless families. Unlike the singles on the streets who have major mental illnesses, these mothers have post-trauma responses. That leads to high rates of depression and then they self-medicate, which means substance abuse. That's the pathway; it's not the other way around. It's not that these mothers are intrinsically mentally ill. They've been beaten up all their lives by family members.

"Little kids watch this violence, they witness it, and they are terribly traumatized. They've seen Dad beating up Mom; they've seen fist fights. We asked a bunch of young, school-age kids what they'd seen. They'd seen people get shot, people get stabbed; they'd seen dead bodies. What is going on here? This country focuses on Iraq and Afghanistan, but does not pay attention to what's going on in its own backyard.

"Post-traumatic stress disorder, PTSD, makes people feel emotionally distressed and upset. They have flashbacks and relive their abuse. These women are just tremendously distressed and they don't know where it's coming from, and they don't understand they have post-traumatic stress disorder. It's the same sort of thing that soldiers suffer who are coming back from Vietnam or Iraq. We see it all the time. Women feel like they're crazy."

In 1996 Bassuk published a paper in the *Journal of the American Medical Association* (*JAMA*). In the study 91.6 percent of the homeless women reported severe physical and/or sexual assault at some point in their lives, as compared to 81.8 percent among the housed women studied who were at the same level of poverty. The study found no significant difference in rates of chronic mental illness between the homeless and the housed, but three times as many homeless women were suffering from PTSD.

"Post-traumatic stress disorder is characterized by intrusive thoughts, periods during which past traumas are relived, vivid recollections, and symptoms of increased arousal such as intense startle reactions and sleep disturbances. These are interspersed with periods of constricted affect and psychic numbing,"[9] Bassuk wrote in the *JAMA* article.

When a parent cannot do an adequate job of raising children, the task often falls to others. Some of the adults raising children in twenty-first-century motel rooms across the country are not their parents but their grandparents. For instance, in 2014, 75,913 grandparents in Tennessee were responsible for grandchildren living with them. Of these, 31,032 were responsible for their grandchildren without a parent present, according to the Children's Defense Fund.[10] It's that way across the nation: some 4 percent of children are being raised primarily by grandparents. The percentage of grandparents who served as primary caregivers nationally nearly doubled between 1970 and 1997, an increase that happened almost entirely in poor and minority families.[11]

People who thought their child-rearing days over with were finding otherwise, and sometimes they also found themselves homeless, Jennifer Cox told me back in December 2003. This was in the midst of a "strong" economy, four years before the Great Recession began. Cox was Shwab Elementary School's designated liaison with its homeless families. It was her job to make sure the provisions of the McKinney-Vento Act were carried out. She was a solid woman with short dark hair who liked her job and worked long days at it. She kept tabs on Shwab students who were homeless or precariously housed, initiating each school year with a visit to the trailer, or motel, or shelter where they were staying.

"One frightening thing is I'm seeing more grandparents caring for grandchildren without having official custody of them, which leads to all sorts of problems. A son or daughter will drop the kids off with grandparents saying, 'Can they stay with you for a couple of weeks?' and a year later the kids are still there. They frequently can't get insurance or health care for the kids. We have a lot of children in our school that have been diagnosed with attention deficit/hyperactivity disorder, or with some other medical disorders that need certain medications. The grandparents don't want to go to court and get custodial guardianship of their grandchildren, because they don't want their children to be angry at them.[12]

"A lot of times, too, the parents still get the food stamps for the children, sometimes a housing subsidy for the children, or aid to families with dependent children. The grandparents are trying to raise those kids and do the best they can by them, but they're not getting any of the benefits. It's tough. I'm particularly worried right now, because we're close to Christmas. I'm not worried because the kids won't be getting any gifts; I'm worried because they're out of school for two weeks, so where are they going to find breakfast and lunch?".

For grandparents who intended to live the rest of their lives on fixed pensions, the responsibility of grandchildren plus a little bad luck can easily combine to devour their family finances and put them out of a house without the means to get the necessary funds together to find another one. "All of a sudden, grandparents find themselves living in one room in a motel with their grand-children, and their money's way too tight to get out of there, even though they are paying $640 every month," said Cox. "Sure they get utilities for that, but that's it. We're talking about an efficiency that's basically just a big room."

John Griswold* was living in such a room on the second floor of the Trinity Inn with his wife and two grandchildren during the time I was there. The kids slept on a rollaway bed in the front area and the grandparents had the bed in the back. Griswold was a wiry, tough African American, a scuffler, a survivor. "My daughter, you know, she just can't keep it together," he told me sadly, as we stood out back of the motel one late-spring morning, the light a gun-metal gray, big low clouds heavy with moisture moving rapidly across the Nashville sky.

His wife was a medium-sized, blonde woman, who walked slowly. She had a pacemaker, and diabetes, and received a disa-bility check. She had a hard time getting up and down the stairs at the Trinity, stopping two or three times to recover her strength over the two flights, and she stayed mostly in the room. Just paying the rent exhausted her disability check, so John, fifty-three, served as the motel's handyman for a substantial rent reduction.

He had gone through a hip replacement a few years before, walked with a limp, and couldn't work like he used to, but the calloused skin on his hands indicated that he had done plenty of hard work in his life. He inherited a house from his mother where the whole family was living, but it had old wiring and caught fire one morning. He had no insurance. The family had been living in one room at the Trinity for the past ten months. His ten-year-old grandson was on the fourth-grade honor roll at

Shwab, and his eight-year-old granddaughter was doing well in second grade. The kids did their homework at school in the afternoons, and John and his wife checked it in the evenings.

Mornings, he swept up around the motel. He kept a Rottweiler and a Doberman in a kennel he had built in a back corner of the parking lot, and he liked to take a break by the cage while the dogs paced tight circles inside it. He held his broad-brush, parking-lot broom in one hand while we spoke, and an open Miller beer in the other. He wore spectacles, and his gray hair curled tightly on his head. He always had a cigarette lit and his harsh smoker's cough interrupted him frequently during our morning chats.

After he cleaned up the motel grounds, Griswold spent a good part of each day doing whatever tasks the motel's owner, Deepak Gupta*, assigned him. Gupta, thirty-five, who described himself as "a Hindu from northern India," came to Detroit to study before settling in Nashville. When I stayed at the Trinity, he had just opened a convenience store across the motel's parking lot, and Griswold had done most of the work bringing the building up to market standards. It had taken almost a year to get the place ready, Gupta told me. It sold just what all the other convenience stores up and down Dickerson Pike did: cigarettes, overpriced canned goods, beer and soft drinks from a cooler in the back.

Gupta was a broad-chested, round-faced man with a trimmed beard and a thick black mustache. He had bright brown eyes, dark hair clipped short, and a gold stud in one ear. Around his neck was a gold chain complimented by a heavy gold bracelet gleaming against the skin of his arm. He was one of tens of thousands of Tennesseans who were licensed to carry a firearm, and his gun of choice was a 9 mm pistol worn in a belt holster.

He said he used to teach a philosophy class at Wayne State University in Detroit. "I've owned this motel for fourteen months and I've made it a better place," he told me from behind the store's cash register. "There used to be a row of broken-down trailers up behind the parking lot, mostly occupied by hookers, and I cleaned all that out."[13]

John Griswold got along well with Deepak Gupta, he said, but he was doing what he could to get his family into better living quarters. He had applied for public housing, but the waiting list was many months long. Meanwhile life was a matter of getting by from day to day. "It's true that staying in a motel is not how you want to be living, everyone in a room, but at least we have a place to sleep."

.   .   .

A place to sleep. To what degree is it a community's responsibility to provide that for families? It is a question that presented itself as soon as the *Mayflower* delivered the first Plymouth colonists to these shores in 1620, and it has been asked ever since. In those first years no Plymouth family went without shelter. Poverty, like illness or accident, was initially viewed as something that was brought on by unavoidable, cataclysmic events in peoples' lives, and a poor person's neighbors were expected to step up with assistance. In the Puritans' Massachusetts colony if ill fortune affected one family, the whole community was bound to respond. Everyone had to be fed and housed, just as everyone had to work diligently, worship fervently, and behave in a morally acceptable manner. These things had to be done correctly or God would be displeased with the entire community. Those who fell into poverty would be taken care of to whatever degree and in whatever manner was necessary to stabilize their situation. If their dire circumstances were due to personal failings, then these faults would be corrected, harshly if need be.

This worked while the number of settlers was small. If a family was homeless, a house was shared with another family until a new home could be built. If a family did not have enough to eat, food was provided by others. For the *Mayflower*'s passengers community solidarity became an issue right away during the terrible first Plymouth winter of 1620–21. By the time spring arrived, about half of the colony's original settlers were dead. One of those who lived to tell the tale, William Bradford, wrote:

> But that which was most sad and lamentable was, that in 2 or 3 months time half of their company died, especially in January and February, being the depth of winter, and wanting houses and other comforts; being infected with the scurvy and other diseases, which this long voyage and their inacomodate condition had brought upon them; so as there died some times 2 or 3 of a day, in the foresaid time; that of 100 and odd persons, scarce 50 remained. And of these in the time of most distress, there was but 6 or 7 sound persons, who, to their great commendations be it spoken, spared no pains, night nor day, but with abundance of toil and hazard of their own health, fetched them wood, made them fires, dressed them meat, made their beds, washed their loathsome clothes, clothed and unclothed them; in a word, did all the homely and necessary offices for them which dainty and queasy stomachs cannot endure to hear named; and all this willingly and cheerfully, without any grudging in the least, showing herein their true love unto their friends and brethren.[14]

With a rich fishery in the ocean and much land that could be cleared and farmed, some Puritan settlers initially supported the idea of bringing poor children over from England. Francis Higginson settled in Salem in the summer of 1629 and served as the first Puritan minister of the Massachusetts Bay Colony. In a letter he sent back that year to friends in Leicester, England, he lauded the opportunities to put children and the poor to work in Salem: "Little children of 5 years ould may by setting corne one month be able to get their own maintenance abundantly. Oh what a good work might you that are rich do for your poore brethren to helpe them with your purses onely to convey them hither with their children and their families, where they may live as well both for soule and body as any where in the world."[15]

The next year, 1630, a fever ravaged the Salem colony and carried off Higginson along with many others, proving again that despite its possibilities the New World was as rich in dangers as in resources. It was inevitable that some of its settlers would find themselves in dire straits. John Winthrop, four-time governor of Massachusetts, laid it out for his fellow Puritans in 1630 as their ship sailed toward the New World where they would establish Boston and Charlestown: "When there is no other means whereby our Christian brother may be relieved in his distress, we must help him beyond our ability rather than tempt God in putting him upon help by miraculous or extraordinary means. This duty of mercy is exercised in the kinds: giving, lending and forgiving [of a debt].... We must bear one another's burdens. We must not look only on our own things, but also on the things of our brethren."[16]

As towns and cities formed and grew, the numbers of poor began to exceed the capacity of a system in which officials responded on a case-by-case basis to the misfortunes that befell their neighbors. It became clear that a more formal arrangement was required for dealing with the needs of those in poverty. For this the colonists looked to the old country. The English Parliament had passed the Elizabethan Poor Law in 1601. It was a piece of landmark legislation that would remain in force for almost 250 years, and the Poor Law's provisions were used as the basis for public policy in the New World.[17] When communities began to organize poor relief, they often applied the Elizabethan Poor Law pretty much whole cloth, and any changes made locally were usually just modifications of that basic structure.

One of the Poor Law's principal innovations in England was that it differentiated between the able-bodied, those who could find work but did not wish to, and those whose infirmities or advanced age precluded them from participating in the economic system. Since then, an effort to distinguish between those who can't work and those who can but won't has always been part of public policy toward desperately poor families, right up to the present day.

For instance, currently in many states the provision of food stamps to "able-bodied adults without minor dependents" requires those adults to perform volunteer labor or be enrolled in some kind of job training class. And in 1996 with the same motivation of winnowing from the welfare rolls those who could work but wouldn't, the Clinton administration implemented welfare reform. The Aid to Families with Dependent Children (AFDC) program, in place for more than sixty years, was replaced by the Temporary Assistance for Needy Families (TANF) program, with an emphasis on the word "temporary." Block grants to states replaced means-tested federal assistance to children and families in need.

"Thus the residual social safety net was definitively shredded, effectively ending poor children's entitlement to minimum forms of public assistance," wrote Valerie Polakow in *The Public Assault on America's Children:* "TANF block grants ... were tied to a set of mandatory work requirements that custodial parents, predominantly single mothers, were required to meet in order to qualify for public assistance. The mandatory requirements have escalated yearly.... After 2 consecutive years, states may choose to cut all benefits whether or not welfare recipients have found employment, and there is a lifetime limit of 5 years on public assistance for the family."[18]

The question is, and has always been, who among the poor deserves our help and how much of it should we provide? Today a sizeable segment of our fellow citizens rails against "welfare queens" and keeps pressure on elected officials to hold subsidies for families in poverty to a bare minimum. What they often do not recognize is the extent to which their own families are helped by government subsidies, things like the federal tax deduction on mortgage interest. Rather they see assistance to homeless families as a waste of taxpayers' money.

Authorities in the seventeenth century devoted considerable time and investigation into understanding the circumstances of the families that were granted relief. When authorities determined families to truly lack anyone able to earn a living wage, they were then accepted as necessary burdens. Many municipalities, "boarding out" impoverished adults and children who could not look after themselves, paid with municipal funds for another family to take them in—the nation's first form of foster care. A related and widespread policy was sometimes called "selling the poor." Towns held auctions to board out their poor, in which the lowest bidder would contract to care for a given indigent individual or family for a certain length of time at a fixed price.

These auctions of the poor often took place at the village tavern on a Saturday night.[19] They were called "vendue" after the French word *vender*, to sell, and they resembled the public sale of slaves, except that instead of chained Africans from across the ocean it was one's own neighbors who, struck by some misfortune and rendered poor, were now being sold off, placed in what might well prove to be unpleasantly harsh conditions.

In the case of cattle, sheep, and hogs, noted one observer, the highest bid was the one accepted, whereas with the human poor the lowest bidder took them home. The margin of profit was usually so tight that it allowed the winning bidder to provide only the minimum conditions to maintain life. "A man who would remunerate himself in such risks, must be a man of great faith in the ability of paupers to live on almost nothing, to suffer almost everything, and to be contented with almost anything!" wrote one observer.[20]

The other principal form of organized public assistance employed in the seventeenth century was "outdoor relief," which meant that if a family was able to provide only a part but not all of the income needed to keep itself afloat, some form of direct assistance would be provided. It might be a share in a cow, a fraction of the profits from a wheat crop, a cord of wood, or a small monthly stipend. Outdoor relief is still an important public policy strategy for combating homelessness among families and in fact is preferred in many municipalities. Today it is called "housing first," or "rapid rehousing," and is most often provided in the form of rent subsidies rather than a share in a cow or a cord of wood. An April 2014 report on rapid rehousing by the National Alliance to End Homelessness concluded: "Rapid rehousing appears to have encouraging outcomes: decreased length of homelessness, fewer returns to homelessness, lower costs per household than other interventions, and decreased homelessness in communities. On an individual level, rapid rehousing minimizes the amount of time an individual or family spends homeless and rapidly helps them stabilize in their own housing."[21]

In April 2013 the state of Washington initiated a pilot program to provide rapid rehousing to homeless families in five counties, and to do so in coordination with TANF caseworkers. The plan was to facilitate coordination between housing and employment specialists. Funds were made available to spend on housing search, landlord negotiation, rental assistance, and home-based case management. Early results were promising enough that the program was extended to the entire state in 2014.[22]

Outdoor relief is still based as it was in the seventeenth century on the idea that a family in desperate poverty is likely to represent an economic problem with an economic solution, rather than being the fault of a parent's bad character or morals. The provision of just enough money to make up the difference between what people have and what they need to pay their rents for a certain period keeps families housed. If this assistance is provided before a family becomes homeless, it is often an effective preventive measure; it also appears to have a high rate of success with families who are already homeless. As we shall see, the experience of towns and cities across the nation is that families receiving this kind of assistance are likely to stay in their housing even after the subsidy stops.[23]

Boarding out and outdoor relief were the two principal means used by early colonists to care for the poor among them. These strategies were not so different from today's alternatives of either taking a family's children into custody and placing them in foster care with a set cash incentive paid to another family to take them in, or keeping a family together with direct assistance.

In the seventeenth century, as now, strict rules were drawn up to determine eligibility for public assistance. Colonial towns assumed no responsibility for the care of a person or a family that could not prove a legal right to live in that community. Even today if parents are unable to show they are legally residing in the United States, their families are likely to be deemed ineligible for public assistance. In fact many parents in that situation will entirely avoid any public assistance that might be available rather than possibly expose themselves to discovery and deportation.

One consequence of the colonial system was that each township endeavored to keep as many poor people as possible out of its precincts. Anyone deemed likely to become poor was not welcome to take up residence. Population in most places was still low enough so that newcomers were easily identified, and it was the job of municipal authorities to judge whether they would be allowed to remain and given "inhabitancy" (official residency), or whether they would be "warned out"—told to move on. In 1670 selectmen in Salem, Massachusetts, ordered a person appointed "to goe from house to house aboute the towne, once a moenth, to inquire what strangers are come or who have privately thrust themselves into towne and to give notice to the Selectmen in being, from tyme to tyme, and he shall have the fines for his pains, or such reasonable satisfaction as is meet."[24]

For the needy families among those who had legitimate inhabitancy—locals born and raised in a town or who had been granted permission to stay—the authorities provided direct assistance or paid someone to care for them. Medical bills were paid for bona fide residents who were ill and indigent. The doctors who treated them would bill the town for their services, as did the gravediggers if the doctors failed to cure their patients.

For the early colonists, the phrase "idle poor" came to hold the same significance as "welfare queen" did some three hundred years later: it connoted someone who preferred taking handouts to working. Some taxpayers began to express resentment that their money was going to people who were capable of working but simply out of laziness did not. What's more, as towns grew ever larger, it became harder to enforce inhabitancy. Municipalities did everything possible to ensure that they were not spending money on people who did not deserve it, and that included able-bodied children. In 1641 the colony of New Plymouth passed a law stipulating that "those that have relief from the towns and have children and do not employ them, that then it shall be lawful for the township to take order that those children shall be put to work in fitting employment according to their strength and abilities or placed out by the towns."[25]

Local authorities often removed children of poor families from their parents and apprenticed them to others in the community, and this was frequently done against a parent's will. For a poor mother who feared that her children were about to be taken, few alternatives were available. One was to move to another town and try to stay beneath the radar of local authorities until she could establish the family on a sound economic footing. This way of life was not so different from that of homeless families today who try to stay hidden, living packed in a car or a motel room, trying not to attract the notice of public officials for fear the family will be broken up and the children remanded into state custody.

Isaiah Brown* was someone who knew all about living like that. The Syracuse, New York, native was working as a long-distance truck driver when a job took him to Nashville. There he met the woman who would become the mother of his child. When she got pregnant, he decided to stay in Nashville, but four days after their son was born in 2008 the family found themselves evicted and homeless.

"I had a job as a short-order cook and a waiter at a Waffle House, doing both jobs," said Brown, a short, stocky African American, thirty-five years old with a goatee and a shaved head. "I knew I was behind on the rent, and I was trying to get the money up. The sheriff's department came and put me out, two days after we got back from the hospital. I knew nothing about it. The maintenance person who ran the place signed my name on [the warrant], and it was the first I knew about being put out. All my stuff was put up the street towards the fence, and I remember people just walking by and going through my stuff. It was a really hurtful feeling."[26]

The idea of turning to a public agency for help was the furthest thing from his mind, Brown told me. He was not about to risk losing four-day-old Joseph* to the state. The family moved in with an aunt of Joseph's mother while they tried to get enough money together to find a place of their own. Then the child's mother disappeared from their lives, leaving him with full custody of Joseph. And, he said, the aunt turned out to have a crack habit.

"[Joseph] was at the age then when he was starting to teethe. It was a huge problem: she was high, he was crying, she was getting upset. Just to get away from the house, I would walk with him to downtown. I had a stroller for him. There's a building right across from the Municipal Auditorium, and him and I would go up to the fourteenth floor where there were bathrooms that nobody ever went up to, and him and I would just hang out there during the day. I kept him changed and clean, and we'd go to a church for lunch. We tried to stay out of [the aunt's] house as much as we could. We'd come back at seven at night, get a little sleep, and be out early the next morning, just as the sun was starting to come up."

When I spoke with him in 2013, father and son were living in a run-down trailer park a couple of blocks east of Dickerson Pike. A handful of balloons from Joseph's recent fifth birthday party were still floating up by the ceiling. The trailer had seen better days, but Isaiah Brown felt his fortunes were improving and he was grateful for the place, which a Nashville nonprofit named Safe Haven had found for him. He was working as a cook and anticipated shortly being able to move into an apartment. Joseph was an alert, energetic five-year-old with dreadlocks and a big smile. He ran in and out of the trailer's open front door. "It was all scary," Brown characterized his time as a homeless father. "Every single day was scary for lots of reasons, but the scariest thing of all was worrying that the DCS [Department of Children's Services] would take [Joseph]. I was always careful not to have anything to do with them."

When a public agency steps in to remove children from their biological families, whether in the seventeenth or twenty-first centuries, it always represents a decision not to use outdoor relief to keep a family together but rather to break it up. Such an action is rooted in a decision that a given biological family is incapable of protecting a child from want or harm. What is different today is that when children are separated from parents, they are not going to be put to work as children were in the seventeenth century.

In the colonies obedience and hard labor were seen as the corrective measures for most ills. Children, even in sound and structured biological families, were expected to work. In 1646 the Massachusetts Bay Colony passed legislation calling for extremely disobedient adolescents to be put to death. No record has been uncovered of capital punishment ever being applied, but it was on the books. The statute's language was drawn nearly verbatim from Deuteronomy 21:18–21. The 1646 Massachusetts version read:

> If a man have a stubborn or rebellious son, of sufficient years and understanding, to wit sixteen years of age, which will not obey the voice of his Father, or the voice of his Mother, and that when they have chastened him will not harken unto them: then shall his Father and Mother being his natural parents, lay hold on him and bring

him to the Magistrates assembled in Court and testify unto them, that their son is stubborn and rebellious and will not obey their voice and chastisement, but lives in sundry notorious crimes, such a son shall be put to death.[27]

If children in stable families were expected to work, this applied even more to children whose families were barely getting by economically. Children as young as six years were expected to do a daily part of the chores needed on a farm, or in a kitchen, or helping out in a shop. "The labor of children was a social fact, not a social problem," wrote historian Robert Bremner, in *Children and Youth in America*.[28]

While breaking up a family by placing out the children as indentured servants or apprentices was what the town fathers frequently preferred to do, it was often the thing that families most dreaded. Nevertheless the priority was to keep children off the outdoor relief rolls and working so that a town was no longer responsible for their upkeep. Authorities had the legal right to remove children from poor families and put them to work by apprenticeship or indenture, and they frequently exercised it.

The terms and conditions of the contracts for apprentices and indentured labor varied from colony to colony, but when they dealt with children they generally called for seven years of job training, acquisition of basic literacy and arithmetic skills, along with room and board, in exchange for a six-day work week as soon as the child was able—usually when they reached the age of nine or ten—and church on Sundays. Often they were not allowed even to leave the house without their master's permission. Girls were usually apprenticed as household maids or cooks. Those boys who were unlucky wound up as field hands, but many received training in a large variety of skilled professions like goldsmith, bricklayer, druggist, blacksmith, or shipbuilder. Often the children began to put in full, adult workdays at an early age, but hard labor was not the only thing they had to endure. Excessive physical discipline and abuse were not uncommon.

Simply taking children away from a family was frequently not enough to pull that family out of poverty, particularly if it was still left with children who were too young to work. Outdoor relief continued to drain local treasuries. As the seventeenth century progressed, growing populations, combined with the expense of keeping poor families in their homes, caused many municipalities to begin considering other means of remedying the sufferings of the poor. Policy makers grew increasingly amenable to the idea of "indoor relief," grouping all the desperately poor together in one place. It appeared logical that congregate housing would be a more effective use of resources, that is, cheaper. If all the paupers and their children were together, supplies could be bought in bulk and expenses would be much easier to control. Another advantage to indoor relief would be that under such an arrangement inmate behavior could be closely monitored, and those who could work would not be able to dissimulate. The first almshouse in Boston was opened in 1662.[29]

Petty criminals, the mentally ill, and the poor all lived together in the early almshouses. Those who could work did so during the day, and those who couldn't occupied themselves in other ways. One of the jobs in which the more able-bodied often were put was caring for those who couldn't care for themselves. Inmates of almshouses nursed, washed, and fed one another. Small children lived among the general population until they grew old enough to be indentured or apprenticed. In smaller towns and cities, almshouses were a kind of boarding house for the poor. A householder contracted with local authorities to provide room and board to a limited number of poor persons at a given price. Many of the adult poor were too ill or old or weak to work, while others were able to labor at menial tasks like taking apart old ropes and picking out the oakum for recycling, or some other unskilled occupation to help defray the costs of a bed in a dormitory and something to eat. The same institution often served as both poorhouse for those unable to labor and workhouse for those who could.

Not surprisingly social theory followed economic exigency and public policy swung toward the idea that the best way to break the cycle of poverty was to place the poor under a single roof where they would learn survival and work skills and get themselves off the public dole. Gradually outdoor relief disappeared and those in need of assistance had to accept congregate housing in an almshouse, or nothing at all.

As we shall see, in many places the choice for twenty-first-century homeless families is the same as it was then: almshouses or nothing. And in today's almshouses—called shelters—it is not unusual to find children thrown together with mentally ill adults, just as was happening centuries ago. Night after night, month after month, year after year, hundreds of thousands of our children have no choice but to go to sleep and wake up in congregate shelter amid families not their own, and some of those families include individuals who are truly disturbed or just plain weird.

· · ·

Four years after the month I spent poking my nose into other peoples' business along Dickerson Pike, I came back for another look. It was Christmas 2007, just before the deep recession set in, and much of the United States was still prospering. I had thought to put up at the Trinity Inn, but there were no vacancies. In fact the place seemed to have given up most aspirations to normal motel-dom. Nothing alerted passing motorists to the fact that this was a motel or anything but a run-down, two-story apartment building. The big sign announcing "Trinity Inn" had blown off the roof months ago and had not been replaced, according to the middle-aged white man who came out from the room behind the office when I pushed the buzzer by the plastic shield. His gray-brown hair tied back in a ponytail, he told me his name was Brian Dunning* and he was managing the place.

The same list of notices was taped up beside the hole in the shield, but one had been added: "As most of our guests are here for extended stays we have decided to do away with housekeeping. Sheets and towels will still be washed. They will be collected as needed." The convenience store was shut down and empty, and Deepak Gupta had moved to Texas, Dunning told me, although he still owned the property. John Griswold and his grandkids had moved out more than a year ago, he said, and left no forwarding address. But there was a new set of grandparents with grandchildren in a second-floor room around the back, and another mother with kids had left just the week before. "Seems like there's more families staying in all these motels around here," Dunning said.

He was right, confirmed Melanie McElhiney, all too right. Federal law requires each public school district to budget a position for someone to deal with homeless students. Catherine Knowles had been that person in Nashville since 1998, but in the winter of 2007 she was away on maternity leave and McElhiney, her longtime assistant, was charged with the county's homeless students. Christmas was fast approaching and the numbers were discouraging. McElhiney told me that the 2007–8 school year was on track to set a dismal record. By Christmas, with five months still to go, she had 1,038 homeless students identified in the system, 132 of whom were living in motels.

Four years before, during the 2003–4 school year, only 306 homeless students were identified, of whom just 33, including John Griswold's two grandchildren, were in motels. In the four years since then, she told me, the number of homeless students in Nashville's schools had skyrocketed, growing sevenfold. Large numbers of families were just one missed paycheck, a couple of debts, and a little bad luck from being homeless. "These are just people who have hit hard times," said Melanie McElhiney. "Maybe they got sick and had to stay off work a few days, and suddenly they can't pay their rent and it's downhill from there. After a while it just comes down to trying to keep a roof over your family's head."[30]

Brian Dunning told me that he was happy to be running the Trinity Inn for Deepak Gupta and living in the room behind the office with his wife. "It's okay for us, you know? You got your cable TV, your lights, your phone, it's all right there. Adults can make a home out of a motel room; you just have to learn to live in a room, learn to cook with what you got, a microwave, an electric skillet, maybe a Crock-Pot. But it's gotta be awfully tough on kids. I have seen a lot of them come through here. I don't think you can make a fit home for children in a motel room. No, I really don't think you can."

· · ·

Maybe not, but every year since 2007 when he said that, more and more Nashvillians have been forced to try. By 2012 the population of homeless students in city schools had increased by more than seven hundred kids over what it had been in 2007. The number of mothers with children seeking shelter space had outstripped the number of available congregate housing beds. Although these children were enduring precarious day-to-day lives, little notice was taken of them. The homeless families living in the city's shelters, its motels, or in cars parked on its side streets were generally invisible to the average, housed Nashvillian. Their very existences would have come as a surprise to people living in most parts of the city, and that's the way the homeless families wanted it, because it reduced their risk of losing their children.

Homelessness in general did not escape public notice, however, because Nashville's downtown, alongside the Cumberland River, was chockablock with visibly homeless people. Amid the skyscrapers, banks, main library, and the Legislative Plaza surrounded by state office buildings, the streets were plentifully populated by chronically homeless individuals. They gravitated to downtown: drifters, grifters, the mentally ill, substance abusers, and people just plain down on their luck pushing a grocery cart piled high with their belongings.

For decades city officials generally ignored the growing population of chronically homeless individuals. Downtown Nashville during the second half of the twentieth century was largely abandoned to the poor. Lots of money was made as developers built out the suburbs with single-family homes and shopping malls for a largely white, moneyed, motorized population. Nobody was concerned that homeless individuals were colonizing downtown. Most Nashvillians never went downtown unless they worked for the state or had public business to transact. But during the first decade of the twenty-first century Nashville's urban planners, like their colleagues in many other midsized cities, found it economically desirable to renovate a badly deteriorated downtown, to do what was necessary to make it an attractive place to live, shop, work, and hold conventions.

What they found was that while they had been busy developing the suburbs, the chronically homeless had settled the downtown streets. Shelters, missions, and services for homeless individuals were in place, and a substantial tent city had grown up alongside the downtown banks of the Cumberland River. Nashville is a city with a major railroad yard and three intersecting interstate highways. It has always had its share of chronically homeless individuals, mostly single men, and a network had developed to care for them.

Over three decades a dedicated ex-priest, Charles Strobel, and an interfaith group of concerned Nashvillians worked jointly with the Union Rescue Mission to create a downtown Campus for Human Development. It served homeless men, incorporating a place to sleep, shower, and be fed as well as providing health, education, and counseling services. In 2010 a new downtown space for the Campus was inaugurated with a 45,000-square-foot building. It had a day room with computers, a lending library, and a wide-screen television. By 2014 the Campus housed some fifty to sixty men every night. Single women or families were not admitted to the shelter at the Campus but were sent to the Family Life Center located in a different neighborhood. It had shelter space for some forty single mothers and their families. Single males with children, like Isaiah Brown, were not admitted at either shelter.

The Campus also administered a program called "Room at the Inn" in which some 180 church congregations around Nashville offered their buildings once or twice a year to house homeless people overnight, transporting them from downtown to the place of worship, where they would be fed a hot meal prepared by volunteers and given a mat or a cot to sleep on in a communal sleeping area. On any given night in winter the program served about two hundred individuals and turned away another hundred for lack of resources. Families with children were not accepted.

In Nashville as in almost every U.S. city many homeless people lived in encampments in the woods or under bridges. Despite the occasional outburst of civic indignation and brief periodic sweeps of these makeshift campgrounds by police, city officials tacitly acknowledged that without the canvas tents, cardboard and plywood shacks, and lean-tos many more homeless would have been living on the downtown streets. The tent cities were permitted to remain because they kept homeless individuals grouped together out of sight, not bothering housed citizens, not discouraging commerce, nor sleeping on the downtown sidewalks making Nashville look more like New Delhi than the "Athens of the South," as local boosters liked to call their hometown.

Nashville also had a "street newspaper" called *The Contributor* published by a nonprofit corporation. Founded in 2007, it was sold by homeless vendors each day in the streets. In addition to providing some revenue to the vendors, *The Contributor* served as a link between the homeless and the housed, and was the largest such newspaper in the country. Vendors wore badges identifying themselves as newspaper hawkers, which by definition meant they were homeless. They frequently stood by traffic signals and silently offered the paper to people waiting in their cars at a red light. They bought their copies at the beginning of the day for twenty-five cents each and were on the streets in time to work the morning rush-hour traffic, charging a dollar per copy. Vendors averaged earnings of $30 per day, which helped with but did not meet the estimated daily cost of living in Nashville. An individual needed $45.41 to eat three meals and sleep in a cheap room.[31] Anyone trying to bring home enough daily wages to support a family was not going to be able to do so by selling *The Contributor.*

Survey after survey revealed that the presence of so many homeless people in the streets and on the sidewalks was one of the main reasons Nashvillians avoided shopping, or living, downtown. City officials began to focus on the homeless population. In 2004 the first point-in-time count was made, tallying a total of 1,832 homeless individuals in Nashville.

This kind of count is a required component of a municipality's application for any federal funds that come available to local and state programs for homeless relief. The counts are conducted by volunteers who go out during one twenty-four-hour period each January and count the number of homeless people they find. These include people staying in shelters and in the streets. Because these counts do not include families who are doubled or tripled up with relatives or friends, people sleeping in their cars, or people staying in motels, their totals tend to substantially underrepresent the numbers of families who are actually homeless.

Nevertheless the 2004 count of Nashville's homeless population was high enough to cause alarm. In April 2004 the mayor appointed a task force to study homelessness, and in 2005 the Metropolitan Homeless Commission (MHC) was formed to seek solutions to homelessness, and was provided with a million-dollar annual budget. Clifton Harris, who was directing Catholic Charities' efforts to reduce homelessness in Memphis, was hired as director of the MHC at an annual salary of $100,000. The city and the MHC committed to a ten-year plan to end homelessness in Nashville by 2015.

It did not take long before the commission recognized that the goal was unrealistic, and it changed the plan's official mission from ending homelessness in Nashville to reducing it. By 2012 it was clear that even this was out of reach, although the MHC's yearly budget had grown to $1.4 million. Homeless numbers had continued to grow and over the course of seven years the MHC took responsibility for housing only a few hundred people. Most of these were chronically homeless individuals, not families.[32]

Across the United States virtually every city has a ten-year plan to end homelessness. In 2008, for instance, 355 ten-year plans to end homelessness were written for cities and counties across the country, yet the numbers of homeless families were rising in these cities.[33] The people who design and implement these plans, and write the subsequent grant applications, often are paid handsome salaries. Many times their ideas and efforts are unsuited to the realities of the situation. Even when ideas are good and plans well meaning, they are often limited by economic or political constraints. The scant resources at their disposal (not including the take-home pay) are likely to be directed at the population of chronically homeless individuals who by reason of mental illness, substance abuse, incompetence, or preference are living on the street, and who are far more visible and annoying to civic authorities than are families in shelters or motels.

By 2011 the MHC had spent six million dollars without much to show for it. The point-in-time count for January 2012 registered over 2,200 homeless individuals in Nashville.[34] In July 2012 Clifton Harris resigned to "pursue a wonderful opportunity that God has provided for me and my family," as he wrote in his resignation letter. He opened a "personal luxury vehicle service."

Will Connelly began work as MHC's new director in January 2013. He was a thirty-four-year-old lanky, tousle-haired, white Nashvillian who had spent more than a decade as a homeless activist. He was a cofounder of *The Contributor* newspaper and thoroughly familiar with homelessness in Nashville. In a move lauded by homeless advocates, he was hired to replace Clifton Harris, and he promptly reduced his own salary from $100,000 a year to $80,000.[35]

Connelly began work in 2013 with two primary goals, he told me. The first was to implement a central intake system whereby a homeless person could make one phone call and be directed to the appropriate services. The second was to have the city commit to the rapid rehousing approach. The initial population to whom he wanted to apply it were chronically homeless individuals who were at risk of dying on Nashville's streets.

The support of policy makers for rapid rehousing is rooted both in its effectiveness and in its savings. This was a dramatic change from past decades when the priority of many social service agencies was to get homeless people to a stage of "housing readiness." This meant that before they moved into housing they would be prepared with tools like money management classes, job training, getting sober, and so on. The rapid rehousing model called for getting people under a stable roof as quickly as possible, then addressing their other problems, ideally with a network of available social services.

"With that old housing readiness model, people will continue to die on the streets because they won't have access to housing and won't be able to get through those hoops," Connelly said. "Housing first basically says that people are ready now, that everyone is ready for housing. We're going to offer housing as immediately as possible, and then once you have that stability, support services will follow."

The downside to rapid rehousing is that it requires an inventory of low-rent or wholly subsidized housing and this was often in short supply, particularly in a city like Nashville with a growing young and affluent population and a small stock of available affordable rental properties. The situation was the same in every prosperous city: between 2007 and 2011 the number of low-income renters rose by 2.5 million across the country while the availability

of low-income rentals remained flat.[36] In Nashville many landlords had their choice of tenants and they were reluctant to rent to
homeless families, who perhaps had bad credit ratings or an earlier eviction on their records. Even though the monthly rent might
be guaranteed by the MHC, many landlords preferred different
sorts of renters and in the tight Nashville market they had no
trouble finding them.

The other problem with rapid rehousing, said those working
with homeless families, was that a disproportionate amount of
resources allotted to it went to chronically homeless individuals
instead of families. Often when politicians referred to the homeless
they failed to make the critical distinction between the chronically
homeless and families that were without shelter. The former were
a disparate group of individuals, made up of the mentally ill who
had no place to go, the old, the infirm, the substance abusers, and
those who in another era were known as tramps, people who simply preferred to have no fixed address. While substance abuse and
mental illness might also be present in many homeless families, a
parent who was taking responsibility for a child had different needs
and issues from those of someone living unhoused and alone.

Will Connelly acknowledged that initially families would be
underserved by the commission's programs, but he added that
his charge from the city was to deal with chronically homeless
individuals. "We are going to miss a lot of families. We're focus-
ing on individuals on the street who are at risk of dying. But I
guess this will be kind of a first step and a demonstration that we
can identify, and target, resources to this particular group, line
up housing, and move chronically homeless people in quickly;
and then along the way we'll work on implementing a central
intake process for families, so maybe some of these innovations
will allow us to broaden this, and include families."

Joyce Lavery was the director of a small nonprofit, ten-family shelter called Safe Haven. She moved to Nashville from Southern California's Orange County in 2009 to take the job, and she had become one of Nashville's most vocal and respected advocates for homeless families. She liked Connelly's idea of a central intake system, a "best practice" that she had seen working well in other cities. What she did not like so much was the MHC's target population. "There's new leadership at the Homeless Commission, and Will Connelly has brought more optimism," she told me in April 2013. "But their focus remains chronically homeless individuals, who unlike families are visible. The devastation of children who are small and homeless can be pretty great, but these kids are easy not to see."[37]

Safe Haven was the only shelter in Nashville that allowed a two-parent family to stay together or a single father to stay with his children. This had enabled Isaiah Brown to keep Joseph with him while he stayed at Safe Haven and the staff helped him find a place to live. "We adore [Isaiah]," said Lavery. "He's a great dad. He's had a bumpy road. He's a prime example of what happens with single fathers. If they lose their housing, the state basically takes their child away. They have to go to foster care. He was on that edge where if he didn't find us, he probably would have lost his child."

Safe Haven had shelter space for only ten families. The average length of a family's stay in 2012 was sixty-eight days. In the shelter each resident family had its own room and shared a bathroom, and there was a common kitchen and dining area. The complex had a computer room and a play space and offered a wide range of social services including help for adults with finances, job searches, day care, and emotional issues. Even with all that, a Safe Haven family trying to get back on its feet faced a number of obstacles besides not having a stable home. Often the breadwinners in these families worked at minimum-wage jobs.

"Many of these low-wage jobs are very rigid," Lavery said. "We've had a lot of clients not be able to keep a job because they had to take a bus to get to work, first to take their kids to day care, then to work. With a lower-income job you have to be there when you have to be there. You don't get paid sick leave; you don't get time off. And, it's even harder to be looking for a job. You can't even get a child care voucher if you don't already have a job."

The ability to work closely with each resident allowed Safe Haven to concentrate on moving people as quickly as possible into housing. The shelter was not open to everyone. Applicants to Safe Haven underwent a drug screening. If parents had felonies on their records the shelter looked at them on a case-by-case basis. If the felony was a sex crime or arson, the person was automatically denied admission ("We serve children and families," Lavery said by way of explanation).

"We're seeing family homelessness growing [in Nashville], but the money is going toward permanent supportive housing for chronically homeless people. Chronic homelessness is stabilizing and even going down a bit, because there's so much attention to it, while family homelessness is set to skyrocket. That should just be unacceptable. We shouldn't have children who live in cars, or doubled up in unsafe circumstances."

For many Nashville families by 2013 the recession was over and life was back on an even economic keel; but for those who fell into deep poverty during the economic downturn, things had only gotten worse. In 2009 about 1,600 homeless students were enrolled in Nashville's public schools. Only three years later, in 2012, that had risen to more than 2,500, according to Catherine Knowles at the board of education.

Some things hadn't changed: Knowles and Melanie McElhiney still made up the entire department administering Nashville's Homeless Education Program. When I visited in 2013, the
two of them were working out of a rectangular portable building, which sat on the edge of a parking lot behind the solid
brick complex that was the Metropolitan Nashville Board of
Education's central office. Space in the portable building not
occupied by their desks and file cabinets was taken up by stacks
of clothes and blankets destined for homeless students and their
families.

Catherine Knowles told me that she did not expect an increased
focus on rapid rehousing to begin reducing the number of homeless children in Nashville's schools any time soon. "We have to
create more units of affordable family housing. Here in Davidson
County, the waiting list for public housing is so long that they've
stopped taking applications."[38]

The number of homeless families had grown steadily, but the
number of shelter beds had stayed the same, Knowles said,
resulting in twice as many people housed in motels as living in
shelters. Some 70 percent of the homeless students she identified
in 2012 were living doubled up with other families; 20 percent
were in motels; and 10 percent in shelters. "If a family can avoid
going into a shelter, they do," she concluded.

Oftentimes packing too many people into too small a space
may prove a way station on a family's road to being on the street.
One out of every twelve families that was doubled up in someone else's home in the United States would eventually find itself
on the street, as opposed to one in every two hundred families
in the general population.[39]

In Nashville the alternatives were scant for homeless families
headed by a single mother who needed immediate shelter. "When

families call in for assistance because they have just been evicted or have been burned out of a home, there is usually some sense of hope in their voice for the first few minutes of their call," Knowles told an interviewer in the fall of 2014. "I listen to their stories, offer information about the support and resources that are available, but most of the time families are stunned that there is no safety net, no immediate place for them to go other than the limited family shelters that we have. My heart breaks a bit each time I hear the hope they had fade away to be replaced with shock, anger, or utter devastation. Homelessness is tragic, but it is a very real event for many in our community."[40]

If Safe Haven was full, and it usually was, the desperate mother on the phone was likely to wind up at the Family Life Center, which was the Union Rescue Mission's family facility. At the Family Life Center mothers and small children slept in dormitories with other families and shared a bathroom. Behind the center was a diminutive park with brightly colored playground equipment. The park had three covered areas with benches and a couple of metal picnic tables bolted to a cement slab. On nice days the women sat outside sharing cigarettes and chatting while toddlers played.

The center usually had about forty families in residence, but there was always room for one more, according to Carolyn Grossley, the facility's director. "We never turn anyone away. We take everyone. We'll even put them in the day room for a night or two while we try to figure out how to switch things around, but we don't turn anybody away. For a family, a shelter is absolutely the place of last resort. They've tried to stay with relatives; they've even tried to stay in bad relationships, in motels, in their cars; they've tried it all. They're really scared until they get here and see that we really care about them."[41]

Grossley, a navy veteran, was a solidly built African American woman who had worked in the homeless services sector since 1986, both with families and with chronically unsheltered individuals. She had been the director of the center since the fall of 2012. "We have lockers here for all of our guests. If you come here there's no charge; you can shower, sleep, and eat three meals a day, and the only requirements are that you don't disrespect or bully people, and that you go to chapel for an hour in the evening. We're about Christ, so we're going to have that somewhere in our mix. It's the same thing at the men's mission."

She was convinced that housing was the key to getting the sheltered families back on track. "Housing is where we should dedicate our dollars. We need to create affordable housing options. We don't even have to go out and build. I think it would be cheaper if we subsidized housing for people. If we were able to offer housing, or affordable housing for a year or six months, we could wipe family homelessness out pretty quickly.

"Most of these women don't want to be homeless with their children. I have mothers here who are holding down jobs. If I was setting policy, I'd go to landlords and say we'd subsidize the rent for whatever time a family needed, and then that family would be able to get training, look for jobs, and do a whole lot of things while they still have safe housing.

"The real issue is housing. Most of the women here want to work, and many of them do. Some even have two jobs. But if you make a thousand dollars a month, you should only be paying a third of that on rent. Go see what kind of place you can rent for you and your family for $350 a month in Nashville. So a mother might go get a place for $550, then she's got [to pay] lights and all those other things. There's no way she's going to make it. It might not be next month, or the month after, but she's going to go under. So, housing is really the issue."

In her first six months on the job at the women's campus Grossley said she had instituted a case management program where mothers were seen within a day of their arrivals and a personal plan was drawn up for what they were going to accomplish during their stay in the shelter. With this in place she estimated that four months was about the maximum stay of a family at the Family Life Center.

Sandra Blake* was hopeful that her family's stay would be a lot shorter than that. She was not happy about having to move herself and her three daughters, ages fourteen, ten, and one, into the shelter. Blake, a short, attractive, thirty-four-year-old African American, had a round face and she looked younger than her age. "I intentionally don't want all I've been through to show on my face," she told me. "I try not to hold stuff in, not to stay angry, not to be miserable and unhappy. I don't want to look like I've been through a lot."

She was originally from Cleveland, Ohio, and moved to Tennessee to be close to her partner, who was in the 101st Airborne Division at Clarksville, forty miles north of Nashville. When he was shipped to Afghanistan, she could not pay the rent and headed to Nashville to look for work. In short order she and the girls were staying in a motel.

"I didn't like that at all," Blake said. "Not only are you paying for the motel, but you have to pay for all your food; you have nowhere to stock up on food; we had the cost of having to always eat out every day, and the baby had to have milk every day."[12]

She had been at the shelter for three weeks and had already found a job at a wholesale pharmaceutical warehouse. Her two oldest kids were in school and the baby was in day care. Because the shelter did not let children on the property without a parent, her kids would go to the local branch of the public library after school and wait for their mother to pick them up. They were sleeping in a dormitory with other families, and she said her whole family had been sick with one thing and another since they arrived at the shelter.

Sandra Blake had been living on her own, independently, since she was eighteen. Although she was grateful for a clean place to stay, she didn't like having to live by someone else's rules. She was eager to get herself and her kids out of the Family Life Center and into housing. "They start serving supper at five, and you have to have your plate by 5:45, or you don't eat. I get back from work at five-thirty, so I have to scramble to get us all fed. At six-thirty they have roll call and announcements in the chapel, and at seven you have an hour of religion. So I have between five-thirty and six-thirty to eat and shower and get to chapel. It's really rush, rush, rush."

She was chafing under the rules, but a strict code of behavior has always been the norm in congregate housing for the poor. The 1735 regulations for Boston's almshouse called for punishment for a long list of misbehaviors including causing a clamor; using abusive language; drinking liquor; behaving lasciviously, immorally, irregularly; or being absent from religious services. Punishment depended on the severity of a person's misbehavior and whether it was the first time:

> They shall be punished either by denying them a meal, or a whole day's allowance, or by gaging [*sic*], or by causing them to wear a collar round about their necks ... or by obliging them to stand on a stool in a public place with a paper stuck on their breast denoting their crime in capitals, for the space of one hour or by ordering

them into the dungeon to be kept with bread and water, not exceeding forty-eight hours, or by an addition of labor to their daily task according to the nature and circumstance of their crime.[43]

For Sandra Blake in 2013 it was not just the regulations and strict timetable at the Family Life Center that added stress to her family's days and nights. It was also the lack of privacy and family intimacy. The same lack that no doubt also oppressed families in eighteenth-century almshouses. By taking away the dignity of privacy, indoor relief acted, and still acts, as a punitive measure. In exchange for daily survival a family has to give up control of its life.

Individual rooms at the Family Life Center were reserved for mothers with children over twelve. "We're in a dormitory with seven other families," Blake told me. "There's at least two kids in each family. There's bunk beds and cribs. There must be twenty-five or thirty of us. Most of the time we sleep all right, but sometimes it's hard to sleep. I didn't sleep well last night. Every now and then you'll have a baby crying whose mom won't get up and leave the room; she'll just lie there like, 'I'm not getting up, I don't feel like it,' and her and the kid will stay in the room. That's what happened last night, and I didn't get much sleep, but usually we all sleep fairly well."

· · ·

In that, she was lucky. I did not get one good night's sleep at the Trinity Inn over the weeks I stayed there. Maybe John Griswold and his family up there on the second floor got used to it, but I never did and I suspect that lots of folks have trouble getting a real rest in those rooms. Mostly what living at the Trinity and paying $150 a week for the privilege did for me was to afford a bad night's sleep.

Whoever rented the adjoining room, behind the headboard of my bed, never got in until three or four in the morning, by which time I would have finally fallen asleep until wakened by their noise, the nightly roistering, hollering, and laughing, with the radio turned up loud to a hip-hop station. After a half hour the radio was switched off and the moaning began. It was always hers, murmuring, exclaiming, urging on a man. The curtains next door were pulled during the day and I never saw the occupant, but I heard the same recital almost every night. The exertions did, always, finally come to an end, and by 5 A.M. I could get back to sleep for another three hours until the alarm clock sounded on the little night table by the bed and I got up, brushed my teeth, showered, shaved, dressed, and tucked the tools of my trade into various pockets.

CHAPTER TWO

Boston, Massachusetts

Falling by the Wayside

While we seek mirth and beauty,
And music light and gay,
There are frail forms fainting at the door.
Though their voices are silent,
Their pleading looks will say,
Hard times, come again no more.

> Stephen Foster, "Hard Times Come
> Again No More" (1854)

The first snow of 2004 was falling along Route One on the North Shore, twenty-three miles out of Boston. Treacherous black ice covered the highway and the morning rush-hour traffic through the town of Peabody was a double line of virtually unmoving cars in the southbound two lanes leading to the city. Temperatures had fallen dramatically overnight and an early-morning snow squall had taken the North Shore by surprise. The usual short morning commute was transformed into an open-ended wait inside a heated car as traffic crawled in fits and starts.

Route One was still an important artery almost two hundred years after it was opened in 1805 as the Boston-Newburyport

Turnpike, one of the nation's first highways covered with crushed gravel. Horses and buggies would have made better time back then than cars were making in 2004 as they inched along the icy highway toward Boston. These commuters would arrive hours late to their jobs. What would be a half-hour drive under normal conditions would take four hours, and the logjam of autos, each with its single occupant, would break up only when the sun shone long enough to melt the black ice.

Outside the Country Side Motel, beside Route One on the outskirts of Peabody, two small blonde boys, both under ten years old, waited for a white van that would have a plastic yellow-and-black "School Bus" sign mounted on its roof. It was already almost an hour late. The kids stayed outside, scooping up dirty snow off the motel's parking lot and throwing snowballs at each other, faces flushed, noses running, each breath a visible puff in front of their mouths. In between pelting one another, they scanned the highway for the van.

When the boys could no longer bear the cold, they dashed into the lobby and stayed there until they warmed up enough to go back outside and resume their play by the frozen river of traffic. Inside the lobby their mother's boyfriend, whose kids they were not, watched over them out the window, chain-smoking. He was remarkably tall, six-foot-six at least, and unnaturally thin. He had a mop of brown hair and a Chinese word tattooed on his long, pale neck. He told me that the Chinese characters spelled "Luck." Looking at him, I had a sense he was going to need it.

His girlfriend, Clare*, who never told me her last name, was a slender, attractive, twenty-eight-year-old with long blonde hair and bright, jumpy blue eyes, who seemed unable to stand still, dancing around as she spoke. Her fingernails were bitten to the quick. She was living with her boyfriend, their baby, and her two young sons in one room at the Country Side. The only country-side around this motel was the unceasing traffic on Route One. Clare's family had been here for "months," she told me, as we stood by the front desk chatting.

Her room was paid for by the Commonwealth of Massachusetts's emergency assistance program and was furnished in standard motel style with two double beds, a microwave, a bar-sized refrigerator, and a twenty-one-inch television. Neither Clare nor her boyfriend had a car. The strip of Route One that traversed Peabody was no place to be on foot, even when there was not a snowstorm. Two lanes ran south and two more ran north, divided by a seven-foot-high metal-link fence that made it impossible to cross the highway. A diner that was directly opposite the motel on the other side of the fence offered large portions of tasty food at low prices, but to get there it was necessary to walk southward for a mile before reaching a break in the chain-link and to dash across to the other side of the highway where the mile could be retraced going north. A strip mall on the same side of the highway divider as the motel, and within walking distance, offered a franchise pizza parlor, which was where Clare told me she sometimes took her kids for supper. The closest thing to a supermarket was a convenience store attached to a gas station at the far end of the strip mall. Sometimes Clare bought hot dogs there and cooked them for her family in the room's microwave, or opened and heated one of the cans of vegetables donated by local church groups and left in cardboard boxes in the lobby of the Country Side and the other Route One motels where homeless families were housed.

She shook her head ruefully. "I never thought I'd be living like this. I had a job working as a file clerk for a corporate attorney who retired, and while I was looking for work there was a fire in my apartment, my car broke down, and I had to move out. I couldn't find anything I could afford. Now my unemployment has run out," she said, adding that her youngest boy had started to wet the bed he was sharing with his brother, while the older boy, who had been a good student, was now getting in trouble at school—fighting and talking back to his teacher.

The luck of the 2.5 million children estimated to be homeless at some time each year in the United States will depend in part on the state in which they find themselves. Massachusetts and New York are the only states with a right-to-shelter law for families with children. Since 1983 the provision of emergency shelter to families in need of it has been mandated by law in Massachusetts, providing that applicants meet a group of ever-stricter eligibility requirements. A waiting list did not exist because once families were ruled eligible they had to be sheltered immediately. About seventy shelters were scattered around the state with room for a maximum of around 1,200 families. In January 2004 these were full and the 525 homeless families housed in Massachusetts motels were the overflow of an estimated 1,700 eligible homeless families receiving emergency shelter. Families had an average of 2.3 children according to data collected by the Massachusetts Coalition for the Homeless (MCH), which meant that every night in Massachusetts over a thousand children were living in motels, the rents paid by a state agency called the Department of Transitional Assistance (DTA)[1].

Many of the children sheltered in a Massachusetts motel had already spent six months or a year in that room. A year for a child is a long time and to pass it in a motel presents a limited range of stimuli. This is particularly true in a part of the country like Massachusetts where the fall and winter months consist of short, bitterly cold days. In those seasons the hallway of a motel is frequently the only play area available to children, and even this is often ruled off-limits by management because motels also take the general public as guests, and few people welcome children running up and down the hallway outside a room they have paid for.

In fact the Country Side, where Clare was placed, catered to a broad swath of the motel-going public, from travelers to truck drivers, who stopped there to sleep before climbing back behind the wheel, to couples who wanted nothing more than a door to lock and relatively clean sheets for a brief period. The motel's cable television system featured a free, in-house porn video channel, but it did not come on until 11 P.M. when, theoretically, all the children were asleep in the single rooms where their families lived.

The night manager was a friendly, middle-aged woman who told me she was a lifelong Peabody resident and made no bones about the Country Side being a "hot sheets" motel. When a young person got out of a car and came in to register her procedure was to ask whether the room would be occupied until the next day or just for a couple of hours. "If they are just staying a little bit, I don't bother to explain the motel's rules to them, that all children have to be in bed by 8 P.M., and that I lock the front door at 12:30 A.M., and I don't ask them if they want to leave a ten-dollar phone deposit so they can use the phone," she told me. "They're not here to be talking on the phone."

She was a short, attractive woman, lively and energetic with an easy laugh; married, she said, to an "invalid" who had a pension that was not enough to get them to the end of each month. Her hair was a soft brown mixed with gray; she had blue eyes and a strong face with no makeup. She was wearing ironed jeans, a white blouse, and a gray V-necked, soft wool sweater. We talked at the Country Side's front desk for a while in the early evening. Then she came around into the lobby and we sat on a comfortable leather couch, slowly drinking the two cold cans of Budweiser that she had produced from a minirefrigerator behind the desk. She told me she liked the late shift. "I put a hard-core movie on the video system at 11 P.M., then I'm free all night. I have to be here, but usually no one needs anything, and later on I can catch a little sleep."

She paused and sipped her beer, then said, apparently out of nowhere, "You know, it's a funny thing. I'd never tried apricot brandy in my whole life, but last year a trucker came through and gave me a pint bottle, and since then I've developed a taste for it. Good stuff, apricot brandy." There was a liquor store in the strip mall. On my way back from supper at the pizza place I could have stopped in and bought a pint. The couch in the lobby was wide and comfortable, and I figured we'd both fit on it stretched out in the cold light of the 11 P.M. movie. I had a strong sense that my advances would not be rejected. But I was sharing my life with someone at home, and one night of passion was not what it used to be. Coming back from supper, I walked by the liquor store without going in and watched the 11 P.M. movie in my room for a bit, by myself.

The Country Side was hardly a place where parents would want to raise their kids. But despite management's laissez-faire attitude, Clare told me the next morning that it was a far better place to be with her children than some of the other motels housing DTA referrals along Route One in Peabody. She mentioned one down the road where the DTA had sent her for a month before moving her to the Country Side. "You can buy crack right in the lobby over there. Nobody's keeping order."

As it happened, Clare's was among the luckier of Massachusetts's homeless families in 2004. Many were unable to meet the

DTA's strict eligibility criteria for emergency shelter. Families had to be at imminent risk of losing their housing, with no one willing to take them in. Income for a three-person family had to be below $1,584.91 a month. That was 130 percent of the official poverty level, and while it may seem like enough to get along with it did not go far on the North Shore nor anywhere else around Boston, where rents were among the nation's highest and vacancy rates were under 6 percent. When a basic, two-bedroom apartment did come on the market, it was likely to rent for at least $1,000 a month,[2] with another month required for a deposit plus more deposits to turn on the utilities.

Even those families with incomes low enough to qualify for DTA's emergency assistance had to provide an additional set of documents, including Social Security cards, children's birth certificates, proof of assets or lack thereof, and letters from family members saying that the applicant could not stay with them. The absence of any of these was often reason to deny emergency shelter. This immediately ruled out many families of undocumented immigrants as well as people in a wide variety of other circumstances. Once families were ruled ineligible, they disappeared as far as the DTA was concerned.

The MCH surveyed 140 heads of families who applied for emergency shelter in 2001 and found that some 18 percent of applicants were immediately denied shelter by the DTA, while another 37 percent were told they needed to return with additional information or be denied. Among families sleeping in their cars or in public places the MCH survey found that 82 percent had been denied immediate emergency shelter. Overall a third of applicants were immediately placed in a shelter or a motel, although it was likely to be far from their home neighborhood.[3] Many families were sent to towns where they knew no one, had no support network, and had to choose either to send their children to their old schools via a long daily commute or enroll them in new ones where they had no friends and were far more likely to be stigmatized as homeless.

The morning I spoke with her, Clare was worried about the fitfulness of the baby in her arms. "I think she's coming down with something," she said, pacing off the perimeter of the lobby while her boyfriend sat on the wide couch and rocked slightly back and forth. "It could be from crawling around on the carpet in our room. It's nasty. You don't want your baby crawling around down there on the carpet where they've used lord-knows-what to clean them, when they do clean them. I try to keep her up off it."

A seemingly small thing like not crawling at will can be an early stumbling block to an infant's development and can contribute to something child development experts call "toxic stress." A number of purposes are served by a baby's crawling. Among benefits to the body are strengthening the trunk, arms, and shoulders, controlling the head's position, and learning how to steer in a desired direction. A crawling baby's repetitious movements also form neuronal connections in the brain that are components of cerebral networks, which will later serve as pathways for things like concentration, comprehension, and memory.

The toxic stress that can accompany homelessness may significantly affect an infant's development. Researchers are finding that a young child's body and brain may be negatively affected by too much exposure to so-called stress hormones like cortisol and norepinephrine. "A brain is constructed over time," Jack Shonkoff, director of the Center on the Developing Child at Harvard University, told a 2013 conference on homeless children. "What comes first in the brain forms the foundations for what comes later. The experience of being exposed to toxic stress gets into the body and affects the development of the brain's neurovascular system. Genes provide a blueprint, but experience builds brain architecture, and strong neuronal connections for things like language, memory, and emotions.

"With toxic stress, there are fewer neuroconnections in the reasoning and learning areas of the brain. Homelessness doesn't cause it. What does cause it is the absence of a sense of adult protection. Of buffering protection. This is not just about above the neck, but also below the neck. The body remembers early adversity like toxic stress; there is a lingering biological memory. It can affect the cardiovascular system, the immune system, or chronic activation of the inflammatory system; it raises blood sugar and produces insulin resistance."[4]

As the richest have gotten much richer over the past two decades, so the poor have become poorer and those with the least have fallen by the wayside. Many of the childhood health problems associated with homelessness are rooted in poverty and disproportionately affect the poor whether they are housed or unhoused. John Buckner, a professor of psychology at Children's Hospital–Boston, reviewed twenty years of data examining the effects of homelessness and he determined that it was poverty, not homelessness, that represented the greatest threat to child development. "Differences were much more obvious between poor children, both homeless and housed, and children from middle-class backgrounds," he told an interviewer in the autumn of 2012. "In short, it has been much easier to demonstrate the negative impact of poverty on children than of homelessness, per se."

In many cases, Buckner concluded, homelessness is not any more devastating than living housed under the negative conditions found in many poor households. "On average I would say that homelessness is a 'moderate' stressor for children living in poverty. It can have an appreciable negative impact for some children, although, on average, those effects often dissipate once a child is rehoused. Witnessing or being the victim of violence, which any child living in poverty can experience, can have far more damaging and long-lasting effects."[5]

How much more harmful homelessness is to children than a housed life in deep poverty is an unresolved question, but no one denies that it often has a deleterious effect on both mental and physical health. In Washington state a 2013 study of ninety-seven homeless families—71 percent of whom had children under the age of six—found that the children had twice as many "serious health issues" as those who were in housed poor families receiving TANF.[6] And more of the homeless children had witnessed or been victims of domestic violence.[7]

In her 1992 book *Moving to Nowhere: Children's Stories of Homelessness* psychologist Mary Walsh conducted in-depth interviews with fifty-five homeless children in shelters, some as young as five and six, others in their teens. The children, many from Boston and the North Shore, spoke to her with remarkable frankness about their lives. Nevertheless, she wrote, violence and sexual abuse were among the most difficult things for the kids to talk about during the interviews, which were conducted in shelters and motels:

> Some of these children have not only witnessed violence but have been the victims of violence. A number have been physically or sexually abused.... Often, these children express a sense that they are powerless to protect themselves and must rely on external defenses.... There are other children for whom the constant assault on their sense of security leads to intense anger and bitterness. Their faith and trust in those around them has been shattered. Since they cannot rely on anyone to protect them, they protect

themselves. These sentiments are revealed between the lines of the children's stories. Themes of anger pervade some children's entire stories. These are children on the defensive.[8]

Children living in precarious circumstances—a motel room, a shelter, a family beset by violence or substance abuse—are at greater risk for behavioral problems than children raised in more stable surroundings. As with physical illnesses no mental problems are exclusive to homeless children, but they have an increased vulnerability to most of them. The mixture of poverty and abuse is particularly toxic, according to David Shipler in his book, *The Working Poor:*

> What is well known is that the trauma debilitates in ways consistent with handicaps frequently seen among the poor. A child who is sexually abused is invaded by a sense of helplessness. If that feeling continues into adulthood, as many victims testify it does, it may break the belief that life can be controlled. Lost is the very notion that real choice exists, that decisions taken now can make a difference later. A paralyzing powerlessness sets in, and that mixes corrosively with other adversities that deprive those in or near poverty of the ability to effect change....
>
> Abuse occurs among the affluent too, but the well-to-do have other mechanisms to propel their children forward despite what happens inside their own suffering. Parental ambition and high expectations, the pressure to succeed, the access to education, the drive for professional achievement all add up to a sense of entitlement and opportunity. Survivors often engage in anxiety-ridden efforts to please, which in certain families means academic performance. The dynamics can be quite different in low-income families, where the abuse is added to a pileup of multiple stresses.[9]

Homeless children are four times more likely than middle-class housed children to be developmentally delayed. In a study published in a 1996 issue of the *Journal of the American Medical*

Association Ellen Bassuk found that homeless children in Worcester, Massachusetts, were twice as likely to have learning disabilities and three times as likely to have emotional and behavioral problems. For some, violence was a reaction to stress that they had learned in their families as acceptable behavior, acting out their anger. Others internalized their emotional trauma, keeping it to themselves, suffering in silence with no one they could turn to.[10]

The burden of these problems often falls on the shoulders of young, single mothers, poorly equipped to cope with them, Bassuk told me in 2009. "While rents rise rapidly, wages do not keep up. In the 1980s, one in twenty families was headed by a female. By 2010, it will be one in five. These are often single mothers with a couple of years of high school who can only get minimum-wage jobs. What jobs there are don't have medical benefits or flexible hours. The kids tend to be sicker and have more learning disabilities and school issues. Many don't have extended families and can't get child care."

.　　.　　.

The sun was bright in the cold blue sky, the ice was melting, and the cars had begun to flow slowly toward Boston along Route One. The night clerk had long since gone home, replaced behind the desk by an older, slow-moving woman. Clare's children ducked in and out of the Country Side lobby, staying in the cold air until their ears turned red and their noses ran, then coming inside just long enough to get warm. "Over the past three months, my older boy has gotten meaner," she mused. "He always used to be such a good boy, but now he'll hardly do a thing I tell him. And his little brother wakes up scared and screaming with his bed wet in the middle of the night."

A van with a "School Bus" sign on its roof pulled up outside and Clare's two boys climbed aboard, the older one hitting the younger with a last icy snowball to the neck. It looked like it stung, and the little boy was crying as he pulled himself up into the van. Clare's boyfriend tossed the end of his cigarette out the motel's front door into snow that was already dingy, and he muttered, "Finally. I thought they'd never come." He and Clare headed back down the hall to her room to pass the day doing whatever they did. Whatever it was, I felt like it might include some illegal substances.

.   .   .

Many hard-working citizens in the twenty-first century resent the idea of public assistance being given to substance abusers who use those hard-earned taxes to spend their days and nights high on methamphetamine, or heroin, or crack cocaine. In colonial times drink was most likely to be the culprit. Over the course of the eighteenth century the sense of the poor as brothers and sisters in need was gradually replaced among many public officials by a conviction that the majority of the poor brought hard times on themselves by their intemperate behavior, and deserved little or no help.

As early as 1707 those receiving public assistance in New York City were required to display cloth badges on their shirts or blouses with the letters "NY" sewn on them. In 1718 Philadelphia passed a similar law, which was followed by others in South Carolina and Virginia. These measures served to initiate "a long, slow trend toward isolating the indigent socially and treating them more as outcast than as neighbor," wrote historian Gary Nash.[11]

By the time of the 1776 revolution indoor relief had overtaken outdoor relief as a solution to the problem of how to provide for poor families. Those who could not shelter themselves were placed in public institutions variously referred to as almshouses, workhouses, or poorhouses. The children of the poor who could not be placed out because they were too young or not fit to work stayed with the adults in these institutions. In 1756, for instance, Boston's almshouse was home to 133 persons distributed over thirty-three rooms. They included seventy-three women, seventeen of whom had children with them. A dozen unaccompanied children were also in residence.[12]

The old and the young often made up a substantial portion of almshouse populations. The sort of person likely to apply for admission was often at one or the other end of the age spectrum. Take this example from the docket of the Philadelphia Almshouse in 1801: "The watchman carried John Griffin, a laborer in the city for twenty-seven years, to the almshouse in a cart, since 'he has had no nourishment for the week past, slept at night in any hole or corner he could creep to.... not being able to walk, and being very dirty and swarming with bodily vermin.'"

At the same time, sharing the almshouse with him was eight-year-old William Thomas who had been apprehended for begging in the streets. The boy explained that his father was away at sea and his mother went out to wash clothes where she could, leaving him at home to care for his younger brother. When they both got too hungry to stand it, with nothing to eat in the house, he went out to beg bread in the streets where the authorities found him.[13]

A ward survey of the Philadelphia Almshouse taken in 1807 found that about half of the children in residence had no parent to watch over them and would have been homeless if not for the poorhouse. Another quarter were placed there on a temporary basis by parents who for the moment could not care for them at home, and the rest belonged to adults who were also in the almshouse.[14]

In 1801 Boston, a new almshouse was constructed. That one lasted until an even larger one took its place in 1822, and it quickly filled. Children and adults were housed together in these various institutions. More immigrants were landing in Boston each year, swelling the city's population of poor families. The heads of such families were often men who were uneducated and unskilled, doing manual labor for low wages under difficult working conditions. If they were injured, or disabled, or laid off, relief was scant and hard to get, and often the family's only recourse was to enter an almshouse.

Many of the desperately poor immigrant families were regarded by the North Americans who were already established here as simply come to drain the public purse or to take jobs away from the native born. Citizen taxpayers resented being called on to provide social services for poor foreigners. They reasoned that if a family was in desperate straits it probably was the fault of an adult's bad habits and willful laziness. Put them in one place and spend as little as possible on them was an idea that appealed to many policy makers.

The trend toward less expensive congregate housing for the poor gained momentum at a time when municipalities were having difficulty collecting revenues to meet their debts. The War of 1812 took a toll on the number of able-bodied workingmen, and in addition the new nation suffered its first homegrown financial meltdown in 1819 when the cotton market's bubble burst, followed by two years of widespread bank failures and soaring unemployment. When the economy began to recover in 1822, just as in the aftershocks of the 2007 collapse the number of homeless families continued to rise. Those who had been in the most precarious economic circumstances when the Panic of 1819 struck found themselves adrift, unmoored, and unhoused, the last to participate in the recovery. Many breadwinners wound up in debtor's prison or without work, their family's small savings from years of scrimping suddenly wiped out when a bank failed. Although the economy recovered, many of these individuals and their families did not.

It was much the same scenario that followed the Great Recession of 2007. "How can you expect to end homelessness in the midst of an economic crisis where the lowest-income people are being left behind?" Kelly Turley, director of legislative advocacy at the Massachusetts Coalition for the Homeless, asked me in April 2013. She was well dressed and neatly groomed, outgoing and energetic, and looked like a lobbyist for the haves rather than the have-nots, yet she had been working at the Coalition for more than a decade. I spoke with her at the State House, which was where she spent most of her working days when the Legislature was in session, serving as a voice for the voiceless.

For many in Boston the Great Recession was over, but for the poorest families things were only getting worse. "Unless you build up the safety net, it's not realistic to think that the numbers are going to go down, so during this period of economic crisis we're going to have to strengthen the safety net," she told me. "We can't just leave children in cars, and in campgrounds, and emergency rooms.

"What we're finding now is the state trying to deny that families are staying in such situations. What we're seeing is that more families each week are staying in places unfit for human habitation. I've been at the Coalition for eleven years, and I can say that before this year I had talked to maybe one or two families who had stayed in a car. Now it's a common occurrence. I was working with one family that was sleeping outside behind a dumpster. A six-year-old sleeping behind a dumpster."[15]

Turley told me about a failed attempt in the 2012 Massachusetts House of Representatives to pass language saying that cash benefits to the poor could not be used to buy "cosmetics," which would have included toothpaste and shampoo. "They really wanted to micromanage the lives of poor people. Saying that there must be something fundamentally wrong with them, so we need to control them. That was pushed back, but there is blame on low-income families for getting themselves into this situation."

There always has been. Almost two hundred years earlier an 1827 report by the Philadelphia Board of Guardians, following inspections of the city's almshouses, declared, "The poor in consequence of vice, constitute here and everywhere, by far the greater part of the poor."[16] The New York Society for the Prevention of Pauperism's annual report for 1821 stated that the city's paupers were "for the most part" depraved and vicious and "require support because they are so." In Boston the 1820 Quincy Report concluded, "Of all causes of pauperism, intemperance, in the use of spiritous liquors, is the most powerful and universal."

While these reports all recognized that the very old, very young, infirm, and orphaned were suffering through no fault of their own, they tended to minimize this, wrote David Rothman, and maximize the fault borne by the poor for their own condition: "This doctrine exonerated citizens from assuming a primary responsibility for the poor, freeing them from a traditional obligation. Since vicious and unworthy dependents were hardly the sort to be included in a community or treated with solicitude, Americans could avoid a burden with good conscience. The poor had changed for the worse, not they."[17]

In addition to the toll taken by war, disease, and economic collapse, the advent of the Industrial Age swelled the numbers of families having to resort to almshouses for shelter. As the nineteenth century literally gathered steam, apprenticeship and indenture waned as solutions for poor children. What grew was the capacity of mechanized industry to use the labor of even the smallest set of hands, but the wages paid to the tens of thousands of working children were far too low to pull families out of poverty.

Two important and widely disseminated legislative reports extolling the virtues of almshouses were the Quincy Report in Massachusetts, released in 1820 by a legislative committee headed by Josiah Quincy; and the Yates Report, compiled in 1824 by John Van Ness Yates, New York's secretary of state. Both were based on comprehensive surveys of the almshouses in their respective states, and both wholeheartedly endorsed the construction of more of them, warning of the pernicious effects of outdoor relief. The Quincy Report lauded the almshouses for dealing with poor families and had nothing good to say about outdoor relief: "Of all modes of providing for the poor, the most wasteful, the most expensive, and most injurious to their morals and destructive of their industrious habits is that of supply in their own families."[18]

The Yates Report, which historian Walter Trattner has called one of the most influential documents in American social welfare history, was no less emphatic in its approval of almshouses as instruments of public policy:

> That the most economical mode is that of the Alms Houses; having the character of Work Houses, or Houses of Industry, in which work is provided for every degree of ability in the pauper; and thus the able poor made to provide, partially, at least for their own support; and also to the support, or at least the comfort of the impotent poor....

Most of the children of paupers out[side] of an almshouse are not only brought up in ignorance and idleness, but their health is precarious and they frequently die prematurely. The reverse is the case in an almshouse. Their health and morals are alike improved and secured, and besides they receive an education to fit them for future usefulness.[19]

Despite the Yates Report's conclusions the almshouse was not a healthy place for a child to live. For instance in the Boston almshouse between January 5 and October 30, 1820, eighty-five deaths were recorded, of which twenty-four were people under twenty-one years. Among them was thirteen-month-old Maria Reed ("a colored child") who died of "teething"; John McGraw, who perished from "worms"; four-year-old Mary Fanning, carried off by "croup"; and William Waine, twenty, who succumbed to "consumption," the same highly contagious tuberculosis that killed twenty-two of the adult almshouse residents that year. Among other causes of death for the adults in those ten months was syphilis, palsy, "intemperance," suicide by opium overdose, diarrhea, dysentery, and hepatitis.[20]

A couple of hundred years later homeless children still experienced more health issues than their housed peers according to the *Encyclopedia of Family Health,* and congregate housing only made it worse: "These children have 4 times as many respiratory infections, twice as many ear infections, and 5 times more gastrointestinal problems than housed children. They experience frequent fevers, ear infections, diarrhea, and bronchitis or asthma. Homeless children are also 4 times more likely to have asthma. This high rate of asthma among homeless children is believed to be due in part to the crowded conditions in shelters as viral infections, common in crowded conditions, exacerbate asthma symptoms."[21]

Another problem for children in homeless families in the nineteenth century was inadequate nutrition, and it remains a problem today. If a family is staying in a motel, meals may be limited to microwaveable foods, to fast food if it is living in a car, and even in a shelter a family's diet is likely to be less than well rounded. A report published in 2000 found a wide variation in whether children staying in different shelters were having their nutritional requirements met, and it concluded that homeless children were at "high nutritional risk."[22]

A 2001 study found that preschool children living in shelters received only two-thirds of the recommended daily intake of breads and grains, and one-third the vegetables. What fruit they were served was usually canned and packed in heavy syrup. Another study found children in shelters to be at greater risk for iron-deficiency anemia than poor housed children and noted that such anemia can result in cognitive defects and poor development, which may last even after a child's iron levels rise back to acceptable.

The diet of children living in motel rooms is even worse than that in shelters. A lack of refrigerator space often leads to drinking sugary beverages instead of milk, and eating precooked foods like lunch meats. One study found that on an average day 32 percent of the participants had no dairy products; 36 percent had no vegetables; and 77 percent did not consume fruit. And what they did eat was as bad as what they did not—too much fat and too many sweets.[23]

Nutrition in eighteenth-century almshouses also was often less than adequate. In 1803 the girls in the Boston Female Asylum were provided a weekday breakfast of "hasty pudding, boiled rice with molasses, milk, or milk porridge, as the season will admit." For the main meal at midday there might be beans or peas with pork, or a broth made of mutton or lamb. Supper was a repeat of breakfast.[24]

In many cases the administrators of the almshouses cut as many corners as they could in providing food and shelter, so that they could put the money saved into their pockets. As municipal authorities were able to order people into the almshouse, these institutions could stay full particularly if the authorities received a bit of the money saved by cutting corners a small kickback from provisioners—so that it was in their financial interest to keep a town's almshouse at capacity.

Conditions inside were harsh enough, but for families who were committed to an almshouse there was also the possibility that the children would be indentured or bound out and the family broken up. Municipal authorities or almshouse administrators generally were quick to bind children out when they could, paying little or no attention to the wishes of parents. What this meant in addition to the natural pain of being separated from the children was that the family lost the potential earning capacity of that child to strangers.

Nevertheless in the early decades of the nineteenth century almshouses were viewed as enlightened instruments of social policy toward homeless families. Conclusions like those drawn in the 1824 Yates Report led to a rapid growth in their numbers. In New York by 1835 only four of the state's fifty-five counties did *not* have an almshouse.[25] However the enthusiasm quickly soured. By 1856 only thirty-one years later, a select committee of the New York Senate deplored the living conditions in the state's almshouses, recommending that whenever possible families be provided with outdoor relief instead of poorhouse internment, and that children not be made to live in congregate housing with adults who were strangers.

Despite the committee's recommendations it took almost two more decades to remedy the situation. In 1875 New York finally passed the Children's Law, which prohibited the housing of children between the ages of three and sixteen in public almshouses. It stipulated that the care of dependent children would be entrusted to either families or institutions exclusively dedicated to caring for children, and that "as far as practicable, a child shall be committed to an institution controlled by officers of the same religion as that of the parents of that child."[26]

Almshouses did not prove to be the solution that many had predicted, and the cost of housing and feeding the poor was not as inexpensive as had been hoped. New York was not alone in its growing support of almshouses during the first half of the nineteenth century, nor in its repudiation of them thereafter. In 1824 Massachusetts had 83 almshouses and by 1844 the number had grown to 180. In 1851 those local almshouses were full and the state had more needy poor people on its hands than it could house.

Three new almshouses were built at Bridgewater, Tewksbury, and Monson. They each had mixed populations of adults and children. In less than a month the three were filled to capacity. In the first year Tewksbury took in 2,193 people, of whom 970 were under fifteen years. By 1858 the population of the three almshouses was more than 2,500 with half this number being children, according to the Board of State Charities, which reported that children were packed like sardines in double cradles and cared for by pauper inmates. The report described them as "a motley collection of broken-backed, lame-legged, sore-eyed, helpless and infirm human beings, with scarcely an adult that is able in body and mind."[27]

It was not until 1867, after the Civil War, that the almshouse at Monson was designated as only for children under sixteen.

Even so, minors continued to live in the other almshouses. At Tewksbury alone, according to David Wagner in a sampling of the almshouse residents in the thirty years between 1865 and 1895, there were over two hundred cases of children who entered the almshouse alone.[28]

Nevertheless policy makers began to recognize that juveniles needed to be treated differently from adults, and by the second half of the nineteenth century it was generally accepted as best practice not to house children with the adult poor. As more public orphanages and children's asylums were opened, the religious nonprofit sector took an increasing role in providing children an alternative kind of congregate housing to almshouses.

Since congregate housing for homeless families was first instituted in the seventeenth century, it has formed part of public policy for dealing with the needy poor. At times it has been the first choice as a solution and at times the last, but it has never disappeared. While support for keeping children in almshouses began to wane by the mid-nineteenth century, we find twenty-first-century shelters once again freely mixing adults with children.

It is undeniable that conditions are better in contemporary congregate housing for homeless families than they were in the nineteenth-century almshouses. In today's family shelter children will not be in danger of dying from croup or consumption, or of being apprenticed, and the shelter will have flush toilets, shower facilities, hot running water, and electricity. In 2015 shelter residents did not have to fear the lash, gagging, or a bread-and-water diet, although they still did have to obey a set of strict rules. Today's shelters are a step up from almshouses. But it is an awfully small step considering that a couple of hundred years have passed.

New York is the only other place in the United States, besides Massachusetts and Washington, DC, where emergency shelter for homeless families is mandated by law. In 1994 Leonard Stern wrote about a family shelter he visited in the Bronx:

> This place was horrendous. The huge, dimly lit, stripped-down gymnasium contained about 400 cots grouped together in family sets along the open floor. There were no lockers. Each family kept its possessions in plastic garbage bags beneath its cots. Needless to say, from the moment the shelter opened at five in the evening until its mandatory "close-out" at ten the next morning, nobody strayed far from their designated area. Anyone who wished to leave, for whatever reason, was forced to check out with the one social worker on site—with their children and all their personal belongings— and then check back in upon their return.[29]

. . .

I didn't know it when I stayed at the Country Side Motel in 2004, but the previous year Massachusetts DTA officials had decided the state should get out of the business of housing children in motels. "We had a peak in August 2003, when there were 599 families staying in hotels," said John Wagner, commissioner of the DTA, when I interviewed him in the winter of 2005. He used the bureaucratese of "hotels" to stand for the motels he was talking about.

"No one could defend having to shelter families in hotels. Our emergency assistance program is a seventy-million-dollar program, in which we contract for shelters, case management, follow-up, support services, and things that are needed for homeless families. None of that was in the hotel system, obviously. It was a great concern that the population of families in hotels was growing."[30]

Wagner was forty-one, thin, earnest, and balding with a trimmed brown beard and mustache. He was wearing a pin-striped suit and a gold signet ring. He had been appointed commissioner of the DTA by the Republican governor Mitt Romney, who said from the beginning of his term in 2003 that homelessness was a problem with a high priority on his agenda. Wagner was from Wisconsin and had previously worked for that state's Republican governor Tommy Thompson, who went on to be secretary of health in George W. Bush's second term. Wisconsin under Thompson was one of the earliest states to implement a welfare-to-work program, and John Wagner was involved in its design.

When he got to Massachusetts, it was evident to him that the system of paying motels to house the state's homeless families needed rethinking. In 2003 the Massachusetts DTA spent close to $20 million out of its $70 million emergency shelter budget housing families in motels at an average nightly rate of around $100 per room. "From August of '03 to August of '04, we were able to eliminate every single hotel room that we needed for families," Wagner told me in 2005. "We developed a more case-management approach, a more holistic approach to addressing peoples' issues of homelessness. This started to dramatically decrease shelter placements.

"By the spring of '04 we had between two and three hundred families left in hotels. We began a big campaign called 'Motel to Shelter,' and added 148 more shelter beds. As we entered the summer, we began a concerted effort to deal with the last two hundred cases, because summer was coming and it would be a lot less disruptive to move them out of hotels when the kids weren't in school. We were able to move the remaining families."

The elimination of costly motel stays meant immediate savings to the state. "Rather than just keep the savings, the administration allowed us to invest that savings in the system. We created a shelter-to-housing voucher that provides six thousand dollars to housing search providers and community-based groups that assist families in shelters, help them fill out applications, look for affordable apartments. We give them six thousand dollars to find a place with a twelve-month lease for a family in shelter. The housing search providers found 207 families in the sheltering system that had a real stable work history. These were people with a regular income. The housing search provider could cut a deal with the landlord by subsidizing some of the rent for a period of time. The idea was that with what it would have cost a family for two months in a hotel, six thousand dollars, we were able to put them in a twelve-month private lease. We're in about the eighth month of this experiment and the good news is that all of those 207 families are still in their apartments."

The fact that Massachusetts no longer made emergency shelter assignments to motels in 2005 did not mean that no kids were growing up in them. Many of the families who were denied emergency shelter of any kind by the DTA wound up with rooms in motels, managing to pay for them week to week. Once they were refused admission into the DTA's system, they were on their own and public officials lost sight of them. The next bureaucracy to notice the children of these families was often the juvenile justice system.

"The housing situation in Massachusetts has not changed; federal housing subsidies have decreased, and the numbers of families at risk remains constant," Leslie Lawrence, associate director of the Massachusetts Coalition for the Homeless, told me in 2005. "The DTA will say that their numbers are shrinking, but this is only because over fifty percent of the families that apply for emergency shelter are not accepted. No one knows what happens to them after they are denied emergency shelter. They stay in a bad place, or go back to an abuser, or go live in a state park if it's summer. A small number can afford to pay a motel room weekly, but most of them cannot. Many of them are living doubled or tripled up somewhere, living however they can. They are hidden, struggling in unsafe or insecure housing situations, and we don't count them because they're not in the shelter system."[31]

· · ·

After talking with John Wagner, I drove out to the North Shore to revisit the Country Side and the strip of motels along Route One. Winter had come earlier than the year before, and dirty snow was already piled alongside the highway, topped and stained with the wet, black exhaust residue of the endlessly passing traffic; but in the Country Side parking lot the snow was as virgin and untouched as if it were in the deepest woods. On the motel's marquee sign, where it should have read Cable Television, Weekly Rates, Free Local Calls, it read instead, Closing Sale—Everything Must Go. I high-stepped through the unshoveled snow to the motel's front door. Cupping my hands around my eyes to block out the sun and peering inside through the glass, I could make out that everything was already gone. The only items remaining were an open folding chair on its side and a concrete block resting on the dusty carpet in front of what used to be the registration desk. No sign of that wide couch in the lobby, only an empty Coke can on the floor. Taped to the front door was a small handwritten note: For information—Room 8.

It was the only inhabited room at the Country Side, at the back of the motel; in front of the door one clear space was shoveled where a big, beat-up 1985 Ford station wagon was parked. It was 4 P.M. on a weekday. An older, pale white man, balding with wisps of uncombed gray hair and needing a shave, answered my knock, peering out at me from behind thick bifocals with black plastic rims, one of which was duct-taped together. When he opened the door, a blast of heat emanated from the room. He was wearing a pair of checked Bermuda shorts and a grimy white T-shirt. Behind him I saw an unmade double bed with a pillow propped up against the headboard. The television was on, tuned to a daytime talk show. We spoke briefly. I asked him if the elimination of the state's funding for homeless families had led to the Country Side's closing.

"It didn't help," he muttered.

He did not seem happy to have someone at the door, nor was he inclined to provide information, despite what the sign taped to the ex-motel's front door alleged. No, he would not give me the owner's current phone number, and he had absolutely no idea what had happened to the night manager. He waved his hand in a vague and dismissive gesture, then nodded at me to signal that our brief conversation was over, and closed the door.

• • •

Was the rehousing of those 207 families who were moved out of motels in 2004 a long-term success? How many of them did not become homeless again? Who knows? Nobody continued tracking them, and it turned out not to much matter. When Democrats won the Massachusetts gubernatorial election in 2006, John Wagner moved to California to work in the Republican administration of Arnold Schwarzenegger as director of the state's Department of Social Services.

Massachusetts's new Democratic governor, Deval Patrick, declared that homelessness would be a priority in his administration. When he took the oath of office in January 2007, the moratorium on housing homeless families in motels was still in effect and the state was not paying to shelter any families in them. Then the Great Recession struck, and by the end of that year the shelters were full and an overflow of some three hundred families were in motels. By the end of 2009 some six hundred families were in motels.[32]

In 2010 the responsibility for providing emergency shelter was transferred from DTA to the Department of Housing and Community Development (DHCD). The Patrick administration trumpeted this as a move that would increase coordination and efficiency and place people into housing more quickly. However, between 2010 and 2011 the number of people applying for emergency assistance did not go down, as casualties of the recession filled and overflowed available shelter space.

By July 2011 the state's two thousand shelter beds were full and 1,793 families were housed in motels, almost triple the 599 families that John Wagner had found so unacceptable in 2003. By the end of 2011 state spending on motel rooms for homeless families had reached alarming proportions.[33] The Patrick administration reacted in two ways.

The first strategy was to fund a program called HomeBase, which would help qualifying families pay rent for a maximum of three years. By March 2013 about 5,900 families across Massachusetts had signed up for the HomeBase subsidies, but the shelters were still full and some 1,300 families were still in motel rooms. Among those families receiving HomeBase rental assistance, 94 percent were headed by females with an average age of thirty-two. Eighty-six percent of the families enrolled in HomeBase had a child age eleven or under, and 55 percent had at least one child under five years old.[34]

The state had underestimated the demand for HomeBase funds, and costs rapidly escalated. In 2012 the HomeBase program was amended to rule that participating families would receive only two, not three years of rental assistance. HomeBase officials concluded that without the rental subsidy some 85 percent of families participating in the program would have housing costs in excess of their entire monthly income.[35] A large number of families would soon need emergency assistance finding shelter, Libby Hayes told me in the spring of 2013. She was the director of the Boston nonprofit Homes for Families and a lean, energetic white woman, enthusiastic, with a ready smile, and dedicated to her work on behalf of Boston's homeless families.

"The things the system has done since 2005 are expand the number of shelter beds, and reduce eligibility. Now, there are five thousand families with short-term HomeBase subsidies that are about to expire. The state sold HomeBase as a three-year program with case management. Because the numbers were higher than expected, there wasn't adequate case management, and now they're reducing it from three years to two years. People took all these risks with you, and now you're not going to even give them access to shelter. To me, it looks like we're on the brink of the system really imploding. Transitioning off of this program is going to be difficult, so I think it's going to be a tough year. One thing that's a little hopeful is that it has also proved a lot. It has proved that you can't short-term-solution your way out of this problem, and really reinforced the need for long-term investments in housing."[36]

Natalia Tremont* was worried that without the HomeBase subsidy she would wind up as homeless as she was in 2011. She was a thirty-one-year-old mother of two: a fourteen-year-old girl, and a seven-year-old son who had "mild cerebral palsy" and frequent seizures. "We've been housed for two years, but we're on the borderline of being homeless again," she told me in

May 2013. "They told me it [HomeBase] was a three-year program. Then they took the third year back and reduced the program to two years. They said they didn't have money to fund the third year. Thousands of families are about to lose their homes and be back homeless again."[37]

Tremont was a solidly built African American woman with a strong face and a direct gaze, who grew up in Boston. In 2007 she had an apartment with her two young children and was in a long-term relationship with another woman. Both her parents died that year, six months apart. Her younger brother took time off from college to come home and help her settle her parents' affairs. He was the first person in the family to have even made it through high school, much less gone to college. On a night out, he was in the wrong place at the wrong time and was fatally shot by someone he did not know. In one year, she told me, she had buried her three closest family members. Her world fell apart.

In short order she was evicted. She applied for emergency assistance and was placed in a motel in Danvers, just outside Boston. Her partner went with her. "Four of us in a small room. A microwave. One dresser, and a whole bunch of clutter. There were bedbugs in there. We had Thanksgiving in that room. It's pretty hard to have Thanksgiving in a motel, although you'd be surprised what you can cook in a microwave." Her nine-year-old daughter was in an excellent school in Boston. Tremont wanted her to stay there, she told me. It was a three-hour round trip by public transport to take the girl to school in the morning, and another to get her in the afternoons. She and her infant son made the trip every day with her daughter.

After two months in the motel her partner couldn't take it anymore and moved out. Natalia and the children were admitted to the Crossroads Family Shelter. Her son's seizures increased and she said her daughter began showing signs of post-traumatic stress disorder. "It was hard being in a shelter with fourteen other families. My daughter was very impressionable and it started taking a bad toll on her. She started lying all the time, making things up; she would cry for hours. She started staying in bed a lot. It was just really bad, she really went through it."

Since the family had been in an apartment with the Home-Base rental subsidy, her daughter was doing much better. Her teachers said she was doing well in school, and she was being encouraged to develop her painting and writing, two things her mother said the girl did especially well. Natalia herself was working as an intern at Homes for Families and was looking for a full-time job in the social services sector working with home-less families.

Initially, part of the HomeBase deal was that if families who accepted subsidies became homeless again, they would not be eligible for emergency assistance. That was modified in 2013 in anticipation of the numerous families that would time out of the program after two years. But the last thing Natalia Tremont wanted was to have to request emergency assistance again. "It just doesn't make sense. It's cheaper to keep paying the subsidy than to pay for a motel."

When HomeBase was presented in 2012, the response to it was literally overwhelming. What it did not do was make a significant dent in the number of homeless families seeking emergency assistance. In November 2012, according to Libby Hayes, the 2,023 shelter units in Massachusetts were full and 1,795 families—approximately 5,205 men, women, and children—were housed in motels.[38]

The second strategy that the Patrick administration employed to reduce the numbers of people requiring emergency assistance, she told me, was not so positive as HomeBase: in September 2012 Massachusetts tightened the eligibility requirements for emergency shelter. In many cases families were denied because they were not yet living in "conditions unfit for human habitation," whereas under previous regulations families who were merely "at risk" of finding themselves in such conditions were eligible.

In 2005 the household income threshold for receiving emergency assistance was anything below 130 percent of the official poverty level. By 2013 that was reduced to 115 percent (including government benefits).[39] For a mother with two children under eighteen this was an annual income of $18,498. Thirty percent of that—what experts agree is the maximum advisable percentage of household income to spend on housing—would come to a monthly expenditure of $462. It would not be easy to find an apartment in the greater Boston area's rental market to house three people for even twice that amount.

"The practice of tightening eligibility regulations is a repetitive practice taken by Massachusetts doorkeepers of shelter in the face of growing numbers of applicants, and it consistently proves to be ineffective in reaching the goal of decreasing the number of families entering the EA [emergency assistance] system," concluded a study released in April 2013 by Brandeis University's Heller School for Social Policy and Management.[40]

After the new eligibility rules went into effect in September 2012, denials of emergency assistance eligibility increased from 40 percent of applications to about 70 percent according to a report by the Massachusetts Law Reform Institute in April 2013. The report concluded:

> Since September, more than 160 families—including hundreds of children—were placed in shelter only after sleeping in places not meant for human habitation. This figure is based on the

Commonwealth's own data, and consistent with the authors' firsthand experience.

These families are sleeping outside, in abandoned buildings, in emergency rooms at great expense to the Commonwealth and the health care system, and in cars—including on some of the most frigid nights of the year. The current policy is immoral, unacceptable, and unnecessary. It is needlessly placing the lives and health of children and their families at risk. And it is wasting more state resources than it is saving.[41]

By December 2012, despite the tougher requirements, over 1,700 families were in motels and the price the state was paying for each room in a Boston-area motel was $84 per night. At that price the state was paying $15,120 for six months. A rent subsidy of $7,698 ($1,283 per month) would pay for rental housing during those same six months. The total paid out for motel rooms in fiscal 2012 was around $45 million, according to DHCD's figures, more than double what had been spent a decade before.

As costs climbed, the state declared once again that it was getting out of the business of sheltering people in motels and planned to phase out the policy by June 2014. Instead of motel stays, increased homelessness prevention practices and expanded affordable housing options would be used to open up shelter spaces. This would reduce the need for overflow motel housing, according to an announcement in early January 2013 by Aaron Gornstein, undersecretary of the DHCD.[42] From October to December 2013, 1,472 families were placed in motels or shelters, a 34 percent increase over the same time period in 2012.

Did Massachusetts state officials really believe that an end had come to housing families in motels? Yes, according to Elizabeth Rogers, the executive director of the state's Interagency Council on Housing and Homelessness, who worked directly with Aaron Gornstein. A qualified yes. "What I'll say is that it remains our goal," she told me in July 2013. "Every day we're being as creative as possible in trying to get to that point. We recognize that there's a major challenge in front of us this year with the end of HomeBase rental assistance.

"Contracted shelter beds are full. Any family that is coming in through a regular process or is timing out of HomeBase and coming back into emergency assistance is looking at a motel stay. Everyone is in complete agreement that a motel is not the ideal setting, and is not the response that we want to be offering. What we need to focus on this year is increasing exits so that we reduce the length of stay."[43]

It did not happen. As 2013 wore on, the number of families being housed in motels continued to climb. All available rooms in the Boston area were filled and families were being shipped to motels in western Massachusetts. By March 2014 things were dire enough that a special midyear spending authorization by the State House of $12.6 million was necessary for the Emergency Assistance Motel Program for Children and Families, on top of the $19.7 million already appropriated. It was a cold winter in Boston and another midyear spending authorization was approved for an extra $32.7 million for the Emergency Assistance Shelter and Services Program for Children and Families.[44]

In 2014, 56 percent of the 11,595 applicants for emergency assistance were determined to be eligible, according to DHCD's fourth-quarter report. In November 2014 nearly 1,900 Massachusetts families, including 3,600 children, were living in motels across the state, according to the *Boston Globe*. The motel stays were costing the state about $58 million annually.[45]

In Massachusetts, a state of some 6.7 million people, 1,500 families were homeless on any given night in 2003. Ten years later that number had grown to an estimated five thousand. The number of people applying for emergency family shelter who were holding down a job was also growing. Some two thousand families receiving HomeBase assistance were living in the greater Boston area, and 36 percent of those had at least one family member who was employed.[46]

A 2013 study by the Crittendon Women's Union found that in a three-person family with a single parent, one preschooler, and one school-age child in the city of Boston, an annual income of at least $67,200 was needed to meet basic day-to-day expenses without any public assistance.[47] A forty-hour work week earning Massachusetts's minimum wage of $9 an hour would total $18,720.

No one was compiling reliable data about the length of time a family would stay in a motel before either moving into a shelter, or housing, or simply falling off the radar and disappearing. Libby Hayes estimated that the average motel stay was about five months. "That would be the average, but I've heard of families in motels for up to two years," she said. "The average is lower because there are a lot of families that go to the motels thinking, 'Okay, it's a safe place to stay, a motel won't be that bad,' and then get there and find out the conditions are horrible. They decide it's better to go stay with parents, or friends, or family, even though that isn't ideal either. So what happens is there are lots of very short stays, and lots of very long stays."

·　·　·

At the end of April 2013 Mary Grimes* was a week shy of marking a year in an Extended Stay America motel a couple of miles down Route One from where the Country Side had been. The Country Side was history—a two-story office building stood on the motel's former site—but the Extended Stay had eighty rooms and every one of them was occupied nightly by a family in the Emergency Assistance program.

Mary was forty-two and looked younger, a stocky woman with a ready smile and neatly braided hair. Her parents had come from Jamaica, worked hard, saved money, and bought a small house in Mattapan outside of Boston. They divorced, and Mary was sent to West Palm Beach, Florida, to live with her grandmother. When she graduated from high school, she moved back to her mom's place in Mattapan and got a degree in business administration from a two-year college. She had worked as a cosmetologist, a chef, and an office assistant, but when I met her she was taking care of her three-year-old son Richard* most of each day and had no time to work, nor money to pay for day care. By living frugally, she had managed to save enough of her $800 monthly check from Social Security's Supplemental Security Income (SSI) program to buy a beat-up 2002 Honda. "The car makes a big difference. I was paying $30 just for a cab ride to the supermarket and back."[48]

I met her in the Extended Stay's parking lot where Richard was climbing carefully out of a yellow-and-black van with a "School Bus" sign on the top. Three days a week the van brought him to preschool for three hours in the morning. He had become increasingly aggressive over the past year, full of pent-up energy. The preschool teacher told Mary that he was acting out and being disruptive. It was a full-time job caring for him every day, Mary told me.

She had married young and eventually divorced. "I did well on my own. I had a good job, vacationed in Paris, had money saved, and a nice place to live. Then I met [Richard]'s father. We both had good jobs. We were enjoying life. We had a four-bedroom apartment. But, once we had the baby, he couldn't handle the crying and stuff. He became physically abusive and I had to get a restraining order. There was no one to help me with my son. I started missing days at work, and I lost my job. I gradually depleted my savings. We lost the apartment and were sleeping on the floor at my mother's, but that wasn't working. I went to the state and they gave me all this paperwork. I filled it in, and after waiting in the office for ten hours they sent us here. We've been here ever since."

She invited me to have a look at her room. It had a kitchenette—a two-burner stove, sink, and a small fridge. The rest of the space was filled by two big double beds and a large TV on a bureau. The room was full of clothes, and toys, and the natural accumulation of a year's residency but still had an air of neatness. The motel provided clean linens once a week and there was a laundry room downstairs with washers and dryers where it cost three dollars to do a load of laundry. Richard sat on the carpeted floor of the room with the remote control, changing channels on the big TV while his mother and I talked.

"I'm really one of the lucky ones," she said. "I get SSI. Many people here just get three hundred dollars a month in government assistance. These are mothers with two or three little children, and a three-week supply of diapers costs forty dollars. Most of them can't work, because they can't afford day care, and there's no one to care for their children. You're not allowed to leave your kids with other people here; if they go to school you've got to be here when they get off the bus; the rules say no one else can do that for you.

"When [Richard] is old enough to go to school, I hope to get a job, although in this area it's hard for a black person to find work. It's pretty racist around here. If we can, we'll move back to Boston or somewhere else. Whatever we do, I just don't want to spend another Christmas here. The last one was hell. It was so depressing. We had to celebrate his birthday here, too. His third birthday. In a motel."

CHAPTER THREE

Fairfax, Virginia

Beltway Blues

> Poverty degrades all men who struggle under its
> yoke, but the poverty which oppresses childhood is a
> monstrous and unnatural thing, for it denies the child
> growth, development, strength; it robs the child of the
> present and curses the man of the future.
>
> Robert Hunter, *Poverty* (1904)[1]

Fairfax, Virginia, is less than twenty miles west of Washington, DC, and it is a popular place to live for those who hold jobs in the nation's capital. In 2006 the Census Bureau ranked Fairfax County as having the highest median annual household income of any county in the United States, at about $105,000, and no year since then had it been out of the top five. In the mornings the highways going toward Washington are packed with commuters' cars inching along toward the Beltway, a sluggish tide of vehicles, most of them containing only one well-dressed person.

It borders on insanity to buck that weekday morning, rush hour traffic in Fairfax for any reason other than a paying job. Nevertheless at 7:30 A.M. one spring morning in 2009 Isabel Sanchez* convinced me to give her a ride from the Anchorage Motel, where we were both renting rooms, to a hospital on the other side of Fairfax, meaning we'd have to cross at least three of those arteries feeding the Beltway. She needed to go to the hospital not because she was ill but because she had a cousin working maintenance on the early shift who was interested in buying the Pulsar watch that belonged to thirty-four-year-old Juan Gomez*, Isabel's partner, with whom she had lived for the past two years. The watch did everything from take blood pressure to count a pulse as well as keep time, and it had cost Juan $140. They were selling it for sixty because with that and thirty dollars Isabel had squirreled away she would be able to pay for a room and a half for another night at the Anchorage for herself and her family.

Isabel Sanchez was an animated, short, squarely built forty-year-old woman, originally from Lima, Peru. She had long black hair and a ready smile. She had come to Fairfax twenty-one years before and held a green card. Her family was living on her monthly public assistance check, but it never stretched to the end of the month. Over the past two weeks she had sold most of the few things of value she and Juan had left to cover the cost of her room at the Anchorage. It was a connected room and a half in an L-shape at one end of the single-story brick motel. It barely accommodated herself, Juan, and her four adolescent sons, whose father she had divorced years ago and who was back in Lima.

For her money at the Anchorage she got three double beds, one in the half room where she slept with Juan and the other two in the regular motel room, where her four sons—fifteen-year-old twins and two more boys ages sixteen and eighteen—slept two in each bed. There was a long motel bureau in the boys' room with a wide television on top of it, the rest of its surface occupied by open boxes of cereal, a half loaf of sliced bread, a jar of peanut butter, and various other foodstuffs. One bathroom served the six of them. It was always twilight in the rooms; each had a rectangular window but the curtains were never open. The air in her sons' room had a density and staleness reminiscent of the inside of one of the battered athletic shoes scattered about on the floor.

A year prior to my meeting her, Isabel, Juan, and the kids were all living in a townhouse in Fairfax, she told me. They had a car and all four boys were in the local high school. Juan was from the state of Nuevo León in Mexico and had been in the Fairfax area for ten years. He had a stiff little brush moustache and his black hair was buzz-cut to his scalp except for a thick hank behind, which hung halfway down his back in a long braid. He was a drywall installer with a stocky body and the rough hands of someone who had hung a lot of it. For a long time there was always work and no one cared that he did not have papers. He and Isabel had met at a Saturday night party given by the friend of a friend. Isabel was working as a cashier at a local Target store. Both were making respectable hourly wages.

Since then, the recession had claimed both their jobs. A few months back they had been evicted for failing to pay the rent. Isabel had family in the Fairfax area, but six people cannot live in someone else's home for long. The Fairfax emergency shelter was full, and Juan would not have been allowed to stay with the family even if there were space. They had been at the Anchorage for twelve days. The oldest boy had dropped out of school; one of the twins attended an "alternative school"; the other two boys were often absent from their classes, lying around on the bed in the motel room with MTV on the television, or gone off by bus somewhere. Isabel received food stamps and $367 a month in public assistance; the money did not last long at the Anchorage. She had sold her car a while back.

With any luck, Isabel told me, as she stood in the doorway of my room and explained why she was asking for a ride, she would get a check from the state the next day, which would subsidize the rent on an apartment. She was already approved for the rent subsidy program, but right now she had to get money for that night's motel room, and she had to do it early before her cousin got off work and went home to sleep. Juan stood silently behind her outside the room, and when I assented to take her in my rental car he trailed along and got in the backseat without a word. We set off for the hospital at a snail's pace. "Lord, make her buy this watch, please," murmured Isabel, as we sat trapped in traffic.

The Anchorage Motel was pretty much of a rat hole, although many older Fairfax residents remembered it kindly. It had a nautical architecture with windows in the shape of portholes and a large anchor on the sign out front beside Highway 50, the Lee Highway. It was an elegant, clean, and comfortable stopping place during the 1950s and 1960s, the sort of place people would put up family who came to visit. A postcard from around 1960 in the archive collection of George Mason University has a colorful shot of the Anchorage's exterior on the card's front, and on the back it reads: "One of America's newest and most modern motels. Beautifully furnished and decorated. Fully air conditioned, TV in each unit, tile baths, tubs and shower, wall-to-wall carpeting, filtered swimming pool, restaurant nearby."

It may have been one of the most modern in its day, but its day was long gone when I stayed there. The swimming pool was drained and the carpeting was ratty, the tile mildewed. The housekeeping standards left something to be desired, even for someone like myself who was not living with children. A small, dead roach on its back on the floor under the bathroom sink was there for the length of my stay and may still be there for all I know. A housekeeper left two thin towels each day, made up the bed with its stained sheets and torn bedspread, and sprayed some kind of soapy solution on the carpet and the bathroom floor.

The motel's quality had declined drastically, but not its price. My single room cost $420 a week. The price of a month at the Anchorage would cover an apartment rental even in Fairfax where rents on a basic two-bedroom frequently topped $1,500. But an apartment required an additional month's deposit, as did the utility and cable companies, and to have that much together at one time was not happening for Isabel and her family. "I've had a good life in this country for twenty years, but the last year has been a nightmare," she told me during the drive over to the hospital. "I don't know if I'd even keep going on, if it wasn't for the kids. I feel like they really need for me to keep going. If it wasn't for them, I might not even be alive right now."[2]

As the rest of the country recovered from the recession, those barely hanging on fell into homelessness. Fairfax County had one shelter for homeless families and three others that had some rooms set aside for families, offering a total of about sixty family shelter spaces in the spring of 2009. The waiting list for one of them was four to six months. A lucky few families were picked up and sponsored by a nonprofit, which placed them in the Anchorage or other area motels while they waited. Most were left to make do on their own.

Everything takes longer when you're poor. Homeless families often have no car and public transport near many of the places where they stay can be slow and infrequent. The coin laundry nearest to the Anchorage Motel was a mile away, a long walk east on Lee Highway beside three lanes of heavy traffic in each direction. Isabel Sanchez's four teenagers produced a couple of large garbage bags full of dirty clothes twice a week. She had a friend with a car who occasionally was willing to take her to the Laundromat, but even when Isabel got a ride, washing the clothes meant hours of hauling, waiting, folding, and hauling again. Sometimes Juan or her sons helped. Sometimes they were nowhere to be found.

To get to the supermarket was even harder. The closest one was a mile beyond the Laundromat. It was another trip Isabel made whenever she could find a ride. In addition to the microwave that the motel provided, she had a hot plate and a rice steamer secreted away in her room against Anchorage rules. "It's bad, the food you have to eat living here," she said. "There's a lot of things you don't get to eat, but I'm not about to stop feeding my family rice and chicken sometimes."

It was slow going as we crossed town against the inbound Washington traffic, hoping to get to the hospital before her friend got off. We made it and Isabel sold the watch. She called her two truant twins on her cell phone to tell them not to go out until she returned, and not to answer the door in case it was the Anchorage's owner asking for the day's rent. On the way back Juan sat sullen and silent in the backseat. I had the sense that he was not happy to see that watch go.

Isabel asked me to help her with one more task: she needed to go by the James Mott Community Assistance offices before heading back to the motel. I parked in front of a storefront office on Lee Highway, and Juan and I waited a long, silent half hour in the car. When Isabel came out she was smiling and told us she had gotten a check for $500 to spend at the Anchorage over the next five days, which would give her time to find a place to spend her anticipated rent subsidy.

I drove back to the James Mott Community Assistance Center a couple of days later on my own and spoke with the executive director, Jim MacDonald. James Mott, for whom the center was named, was an African American attorney and community activist in the Fairfax area in the 1960s. MacDonald explained that the center was nondenominational and was funded both publicly and privately, operating on an annual budget of less than half a million dollars. He added that a good deal of his working day was taken up with fund-raising.

MacDonald was sixty, a tall man with salt-and-pepper hair brushed back and a trimmed beard. "We feed a hundred families a week, and we also help people with their rent and utility bills," he told me. "We never have a shortage of clients, and we have new ones come in every day. Fairfax County is one of the richest places in the world, but there's a whole underbelly of disadvantaged people.

"Most of our clients are people who really want to work; they just can't find it. We need more housing and we need more jobs. I've had people with master's and doctorates come in here looking for assistance, although the average client is a young, black mother of two or three kids, who has never been married. One thing about most of the folks who come in here is that their faith seems to be strong; they are down and out, but their faith is stronger than most people's."

•   •   •

Both currently and historically, minorities and immigrants have made up a disproportionate number of the nation's homeless families. Now as always these groups make the lowest wages and the jobs they hold are frequently the most precarious. They are the first to suffer in economic downturns and the last to recover. African Americans and Latinos are considerably overrepresented among the current population of homeless families, just as they are overrepresented in the number of American families living in poverty.

A study in Milwaukee found that women from black neighborhoods in the city accounted for 9.6 percent of the population but 30 percent of the evictions, an event that often immediately precedes homelessness.[3] In 2010 the U.S. Census found that 44 percent of black single-parent families lived below the poverty line, while only 22 percent of white single-parent families did so. In that same year one of every 141 black family members stayed in a homeless shelter, compared to one in 990 members of white families, and while African American families accounted for just 12.3 percent of the U.S. population, they represented 38.8 percent of the population in homeless shelters. Meanwhile white families made up 63.7 percent of the country but white people accounted for just 28.6 percent of the shelter population.[4]

A 2012 report concluded: "Due to interrelated barriers to economic self-sufficiency and prosperity, such as institutionalized discrimination and multigenerational poverty, black families have unequal access to decent housing, employment, and education. These social exclusions leave blacks more likely to have smaller financial reserves to fall back on in emergency situations; reside in poor, segregated, and unsafe neighborhoods that lack community resources; and experience homelessness."[5]

While some 13 percent of whites lived below the federal poverty line, 35 percent of blacks did so, and 33 percent of Hispanics.[6] One in every 353 Latinos had stayed in a shelter.[7] Texas in 2008 was ranked by the National Center on Family Homelessness as having the most severe child homelessness problem in the country. While no figures were available for the ethnic makeup of those homeless children, some 56 percent of people living below the poverty line in Texas were Hispanic.[8]

It is generally agreed that there are many more homeless Latino families than shelter counts reflect. They are living doubled and tripled up with friends or families, because for many Latinos it is unthinkable to let people close to them enter a shelter.[9] Another reason for the undercount is that many undocumented heads of immigrant families are reluctant to seek social services when they are facing homelessness. Those that do, often find that the lack of a Social Security number or a green card means they are ineligible. They may not be able to obtain things like food stamps or TANF benefits, depending on the state in which they are living.

Immigrant families frequently rely on one or two incomes from the most precarious and poorly paid employment. The jobs most often held by Latino immigrants are day labor, construction, restaurant work, cleaning, painting, or gardening.[10] In economic downturns they will be the first to go. If they must seek help outside the family, they are likely to do so from a church or religious-based nonprofit where their legal status will not be a factor in a decision about whether to offer assistance. These families are not likely to be included in official counts of homeless families.

No one knows the number of homeless, undocumented immigrant heads-of-households, but these people face even more barriers in their struggles to pull their families out of homelessness than white or black North Americans. Language often presents a considerable difficulty for them, and in addition they may be trying not to call attention to themselves or their situations.

They do what they can to become the most invisible people in the invisible nation, and it is likely to take a toll on their children.

. . .

In the nineteenth century, as in the twenty-first, low-wage jobs were relatively plentiful in the United States compared to many poorer countries, and people set out in great numbers from their impoverished European homelands to come to America, bringing little more than meager savings and the clothes on their backs. As the Industrial Age was born and prospered, immigration became an attractive alternative to a life of grinding poverty in the old countries.

The crossing was expensive and dangerous, just as it is today for those trying to reach Europe or North America, who may pay a lot of money for someone to smuggle them only to die of thirst in the deserts of Arizona or drown in the Mediterranean when a crowded launch overturns. In the nineteenth century it was disease that carried off many a ship's passengers before the New World was reached. Those immigrants who survived the crossing often landed in the United States with fewer family members than they set out with, having watched their spouses or children die on the high seas.

Even if a family managed to reach the United States intact, they were likely to face a host of troubles. Frequently they had to struggle with a foreign language, a distinct culture, and customs that were completely different from any they had known. Those lucky enough to find a job often endured abysmal working conditions. The tastes, smells, and sounds they had lived with all their lives were suddenly gone, and what had taken their place was incomprehensible to many.

Newly arrived immigrant families frequently found themselves homeless. As early as the 1790s one in every three almshouse residents was born in a foreign country.[11] Then as now immigrants made up a disproportionate number of homeless families. For many homegrown citizens in the nineteenth century this increasing population of poor people from foreign places combined in their minds with the growing concept of the poor as a lazy lot looking for handouts. The immigrants, they believed, had come not to work but only to be eligible for the dole so that they would not have to labor and could live on public charity.

Great numbers of the new arrivals were Roman Catholics, at first from Ireland then after the Civil War from southern Europe. The native-born citizens were almost entirely Protestants and they viewed the Catholics as a morally lax bunch of people, inclined to breed like rabbits and with a dubious work ethic. The results of all that breeding, they complained, were poor families to support with taxpayers' money.

By 1850, 35 percent of Boston's population of 136,881 was born in a foreign country.[12] A state commission's report noted that the expense of public assistance had tripled in the past decade. While acknowledging a responsibility for families in desperate poverty, the report stressed that the real task was to keep aid to a bare minimum: "The community should be satisfied ... that they have done their whole duty to a foreign pauper when they have made provision for him to preserve his health, and that the coarsest and cheapest food, and the humblest clothing and shelter consistent with this primary object, are all he has a right to claim."[13]

Fortunately for the children in the homeless families of "foreign paupers," not everyone in the nation subscribed to the idea of providing them with only the barest necessities for staying alive and leaving them to whatever their fates. The nineteenth century witnessed a proliferation of "child-saving" agencies across the country. Unfortunately they frequently practiced racial segregation—assisting white children while leaving black families to fend for themselves.

In nineteenth-century Boston as elsewhere a growing number of religious charities undertook ministering to poor, homeless, white children of immigrants, whose parents were either dead or unable to care for them. At first these charities were primarily Protestant based. Among the earliest was one that owed its existence to a twelve-year-old girl, Fannie Merrill, the daughter of the Reverend George Merrill, a Unitarian Sunday school superintendent and prominent Bostonian. One Sunday as father and daughter were walking to church, they passed through a poor neighborhood where some poor, ragged children were playing in the street. Fannie is said to have asked her father, "Can't we do something for these little things?"

Inspired by his daughter's concern, so the story goes, her father founded the Boston Children's Mission in 1849. Since indenture and apprenticeship were disappearing in the big cities, the process of placing out children locally, one by one, was too slow for Merrill's taste. He came up with the idea of placing groups of children farther afield. Small towns and farms in New England were often short handed, and Merrill began organizing and sending two or three trainloads of children to these places each year.[14]

The Children's Mission was the first child welfare organization to send agents out into the streets looking for homeless children. They did not have to look too hard. Many children from poor immigrant families preferred to live a precarious existence on the streets rather than submit to the rules and regulations of either public or private congregate housing. More and more children were living by their wits, homeless or virtually so; these kids had escaped from dysfunctional families or an almshouse. On the other hand, some of the street kids and their parents liked the sound of the deal offered by the Children's Mission agents: free transportation to a farm where they would work in exchange for room, board, and a life free of the day-to-day scuffle of survival in alleys and on street corners. Eventually Merrill sent groups of thirty to fifty children throughout New England.

The number of immigrants declined between 1861 and 1865 as the ongoing Civil War discouraged many Europeans from coming to North America. However, the war created its own hardships and greatly increased the number of young, American-born widows and their families needing assistance. The Civil War years were particularly difficult for some children. Boys under sixteen were occasionally found on the battlefields in both armies. Even those children who stayed at home often had to step up and do an adult's work. The war years brought hard times for many and filled the almshouses with homeless families.[15] Children took whatever jobs they could find in order to keep their families housed. In rural areas this meant boys and girls had to work in the fields, and in cities it meant working in factories.

After the Civil War a new wave of immigrants from southern Europe—Italy, Greece, and Portugal—began to arrive in ever greater numbers.[16] Whenever possible children from homeless families were housed in orphanages rather than adult almshouses. The first orphanages were mostly Protestant, but Jewish and Roman Catholic orphanages soon followed them. It was that or give up their poorest children—of whom both religions had many—to the care of Protestants.

Orphanages in many cities were racially segregated. The first orphanage for African American children was opened in Philadelphia in 1822.[17] A new home was constructed in 1838 as the numbers of orphans overwhelmed the capacity of the first one. Before it could be occupied an antiabolitionist, white mob burned it down. In New York City a group of Quakers in 1836 opened the Association for the Benefit of Colored Orphans, popularly known as the Colored Orphans Asylum. It filled up quickly and generally stayed that way. On a hot July evening in 1863 the building was attacked and burned to the ground by an angry, white mob protesting the Civil War draft and out to get any black people they could find. Fortunately the asylum's matrons had the presence of mind to lead the 233 children in residence at the time out the back door before the fire started, and no lives were lost. By 1850 colored orphan asylums had opened in Providence and Cincinnati.

The tenor of life inside an orphanage was determined as much by the employees of a given institution as by race or religious denomination. In some of them rules were not excessively strict and children—usually under fourteen—were treated well, educated, and prepared for a trade. In others costs were cut to the bone and children were put to work as soon as possible. Cruel behavior was not restricted to any religious group. Historian Priscilla Ferguson recounted: "One youngster, who lived in the Hebrew Orphan Asylum in New York in the 1860s and 1870s, recalled that a boy who wet his bed 'was taken time and again from his bed in the early morning, placed in the bath and the cold shower turned on him, being threatened if he moved with a rawhide by the Warden, his screams could be heard all over the building and it was only when his cries became faint that he was released but not before he received a few welts from the rawhide.'"[18]

As late as 1910 Hastings Hart, who had served as president of the National Conference of Charities and Correction, wrote:

> There still survive orphan asylums where children are kept in uniform ... where lice and bedbugs prevail; where food is meager and of inferior quality ... where sleeping rooms are insanitary; where thin beds let the tender bodies down upon hard wooden slats; where cuffs and abuse are more freely distributed than kind words.
>
> But on the other hand there are children's homes and orphan asylums where tenderness and love prevail.[19]

And so it went down through the history of orphanages. Forty years later, in a South Dakota orphanage for Native American children run by the Roman Catholic church, one adult remembered being molested and raped by the head priest during the 1950s and being completely unable to tell anyone what was happening. "It was like a horror movie in which people walk by each other but can't communicate."[20]

The idea that caring for homeless children should fall to a religious institution appears in one form or another over the entire history of Europeans in North America. It is an idea still in practice. Volunteers from churches in communities across the nation help to feed homeless families on a regular basis, and in many cities congregations open their facilities as homeless shelters one or two nights a year.

Fairfax County's places of worship had organized the year so that every evening a hot meal would be provided to the homeless. The program was administered by FACETS, a Fairfax nonprofit which had served the homeless since 1988. Over the course of 2008 FACETS was responsible for distributing nearly forty thousand hot meals. Congregations assumed financial responsibility for certain dates, and volunteers bought the food, prepared the evening meals in the church kitchen, and delivered them to the homeless.

The first and third Mondays of each month belonged to the Fairfax Presbyterian Church. It was a large brick building located behind a business park in a stand of northern Virginia woods. The church grounds were neatly groomed and the place had the feel of a college campus. The volunteer congregation members had things well in hand on the night in 2009 when I visited. The church kitchen was of an industrial size, and 120 small brown sacks were prepared and ready to be delivered, each with a Styrofoam container of beef stew, an apple, a packet of celery sticks, two Little Debbie Creme Pies, a paper napkin, and a spoon. The beef stew had been bought in a dozen six-pound, ten-ounce cans with $146 in church funds, heated, and put in the containers, where it would stay hot.

Leo Schenck was driving the church van that night. A retired seventy-year-old, he and a helper made four stops including the Anchorage Motel, where thirty-three meals were handed out. In addition to the Anchorage we went to another motel and two parking lots beside woods. When we arrived at each stop, Schenck gave the distinctive three-note honk used each night by the volunteer drivers, and immediately people materialized to form a line. We distributed the paper bags from the back of the van to all comers, no questions asked. Anyone who asked for more than one sack was accommodated until the food ran out.

A good thing we were not doing the same thing in Florida, where we could have been arrested. For climatic reasons Florida is the state, along with California, where the largest percentage of the nation's homeless live. In a dozen Florida cities (and a dozen more in California) it was illegal to feed the homeless, punishable by hefty fines or jail time. In November 2014 Arnold Abbott, a ninety-year-old director of a local interfaith volunteer organization in Fort Lauderdale, was arrested twice in one week for handing out meals in a public park to homeless individuals and families.[21]

These laws reflected a move in numerous cities to deal with increasing numbers of homeless people by criminalizing homelessness. In 2011 thirty-seven cities had laws on the books prohibiting people from sleeping in vehicles. By the end of 2014 the number had more than doubled to eighty-one cities. City officials, desperate to cleanse their streets of homeless individuals, tried to outlaw homelessness. The rationale for banning food sharing was that it promoted the gathering of homeless individuals in a public place where they would be nuisances, loitering, urinating, or sleeping in public, panhandling, or otherwise molesting passers-by. While these regulations were usually designed with the intent of reducing the number of visible, chronically homeless individuals, they affected families as well. When food sharing was prohibited, both individuals and families went hungry.

Across the nation the distribution of food to the homeless in public places was prohibited in more and more cities, from Dallas to Birmingham to Wilmington, North Carolina, even as more and more people in these places went hungry. Ninety-one percent of twenty-five cities surveyed in 2013 reported an increase in first-time requests for food assistance, and 66 percent of these cities reported that a lack of resources had meant turning away people who requested food assistance sometime during the year.[22]

·   ·   ·

The children of poor nineteenth-century immigrants often faced futures filled with hunger and want. While many families had immigrated for the express purpose of offering their children better lives, in many cases the children had to work at whatever they could find in order to help put food on the table and they were effectively condemned to lives of low-wage misery. By 1900 some two million of the nation's children between the ages of ten and fifteen were working in factories, on farms, or in urban streets, while only 8 percent of eligible youth attended a high school.[23] For employers child labor offered a huge pool of potential workers whom they could hire and fire at will, paying low wages in the meantime.

While many urban children found work in factories, many others labored in what were called "street trades." The streets were their homes, their playgrounds, and their workplaces. Often the boys worked as "newsies," selling a daily newspaper; or as bootblacks, shining shoes; or as peddlers, wood and coal gatherers, garbage dump scavengers, or market boys who hung around the markets and did whatever lifting, carrying, or hauling for which anyone wanted to pay them. Girls frequently sold flowers, pins, or notions.

At the same time the child reform movement was coalescing. Before the mid-nineteenth century children were seen as small adults, each carrying a burden of original sin, and they were generally undifferentiated from the grown people around them. However, that changed over the decades and by 1900 it was widely accepted that childhood was a different state of being from adulthood, with its own needs and dangers, and that children needed special protection under the law.

In 1875 New York passed the Children's Law, which prohibited housing children between the ages of three and sixteen in public almshouses, mandating that they be placed either with families or in institutions exclusively for children. This law also stipulated that "as far as practicable, a child should be committed to an institution controlled by officers of the same religion as that of the parents of that child."[24]

The number of orphanages grew rapidly. In 1860 the United States had 124 orphan asylums and by 1888 there were 613 of them housing some fifty thousand orphans.[25] These orphanages were either public, funded by the state or municipality in which they were located, or sponsored by charitable groups, often religious in nature. Whether public or charitable they received no federal assistance. The federal government had made it clear that such expenses were to be met at the state and local levels, or they would not be met. Washington, DC, recognized no responsibility toward the nation's homeless children and local oversight of conditions in orphanages varied greatly.

The federal government's policy had been spelled out with a presidential veto in 1854. That year Congress passed the Bill for the Benefit of the Indigent Insane, which set aside more than ten million acres of federal land for states to use in the construction of asylums for the mentally ill as well as the deaf and the blind. President Franklin Pierce vetoed the legislation declaring: "If Congress has the power to make provision for the indigent insane it has the same power to provide for the indigent who are not insane; and thus to transfer to the Federal Government the charge of all poor in all the states.... I cannot find any authority in the Constitution for making the Federal Government the great almoner of public charity throughout the United States."[26]

This set the tone for the federal response to children living in poverty for the next half century. No assistance would be forthcoming from Washington. Each state was entirely responsible for its poor families and for measures to alleviate their plights. Many of the states budgeted as little as possible toward aiding the poor and by the end of the nineteenth century, while states still maintained some public workhouses and orphanages, services for extremely poor families were often in the hands of nonprofit charitable organizations often affiliated with a particular denomination.

.   .   .

In 2009 parents in Fairfax who were having a hard time keeping their families intact without a place to stay often found themselves turning for assistance to FACETS. This nonprofit had enlisted about thirty churches, each willing to open its facilities to shelter the homeless for a week during winter in a hypothermia prevention program. FACETS also hosted a number of after-school programs for youngsters and offered classes to adults in things like financial management.

When I visited Fairfax in the spring of 2009, FACETS officials were alarmed by the surge in the numbers of homeless families. Tycie Young, a thirty-year-old blonde woman who was the nonprofit's communications director, told me: "What we're seeing over the past year is a little scary. Just over the past month, there has been an eighteen percent increase in the number of people we're serving with our meals. Over the past year, it has been a twenty-five percent increase. What's even more worrying is that much of the increase has been families who were homeless for the first time ever. And among these first-time homeless families, there's been a big increase in two-parent families. About sixty-four percent of the adults in the families we serve are employed."[27]

FACETS had helped the county's homeless through good times and bad. Nevertheless Tycie Young, who had been with the nonprofit for almost three years, said she worried the situation had reached unprecedented proportions. "Another factor in all these increases is the way we have had to work with more and more immigrants. And I'm not just talking Spanish-speakers, but people from Somalia, Sudan, Arab-speakers, people from all over. They're here, and they can't speak any English. We have a translation service we use, and we try to find out what they need and to make them aware of what's available. The kids are often surprisingly resilient, as long as they have a parent to hand and a school to go to. Kids can be pretty self-sufficient."

This ability of kids to adapt to their circumstances is nothing new. In the mid-nineteenth century the streets of the nation's cities had a growing population of self-sufficient, dirt-poor children living in them, making their way from day to day as best they could. In 1853 a young, Yale-educated Protestant minister, Charles Loring Brace, inspired by the work of Merrill's group in Boston, decided he would devote his life to the poor children of New York City. He believed that the adult poor were practically impossible to reform but that children were salvageable, still free of the bonds of vice. He founded the New York Children's Aid Society (CAS) to minister to the needs of the juveniles often referred to as "street Arabs" because of their ceaseless wanderings in the streets.

In 1854 Brace initiated the two programs that would be the cornerstones of the society's work. He opened the first Newsboy's Lodging House and sent the first "orphan train" westward, carrying New York City street children to be placed out in rural America. The Newsboy's Lodging House was a shelter for the city's newsboys, who were working children as young as eight years, often homeless, hawking the city's penny newspapers in the streets. Up until then many of them had no choice other than to spend nights outside in the most sheltered place they could find, huddling up to sleep in empty lots or the corner of a back alley during summer, or on warm steam grates in the winter. By the 1850s selling newspapers had become the number-one occupation for boys under thirteen. They bought their bundles of newspapers without a returns policy, meaning that they sold all they had or kept trying until it was so late that any unsold papers were only good for sleeping under.

In the last half of the nineteenth century newsboys were a familiar sight in many cities, offering their papers until late at night. They enjoyed a certain vogue as the heroes of popular novels written by the likes of Horatio Alger Jr., in which they rose from rags to riches, but the reality of a hardscrabble life in the streets was far different according to the CAS: "Many of [the newsboys] had no home, and slept under steps, in boxes, or in corners of the printing house stairways. Others lodged in filthy beds, in the back-side of low groceries. They were dirty, ragged, impudent, and obscene; and continually, from want of means or for petty crimes, were falling into the station-houses or the prisons. Their money, which was easily earned, was more quickly spent in gambling, theatres, and low pleasures for which, though children, they had a man's aptitude."[28]

The society opened the first Newsboy's Lodging House over the offices of *The Sun* newspaper in 1854. That first year was a success according to the society's 1855 report: "There have been 6,872 lodgers in the house during the year, and 408 different boys. . . . The newsboys are certainly not now 'model little boys'; but they are greatly changed from their condition when we first knew them. They come regularly to our evening school, and the informal religious meeting on Sunday evenings. They wear clean shirts and clean clothes. Gambling and drinking have been much left off by them."

Just how many boys worked as newsboys across the country was impossible to estimate, but every city with a daily newspaper had them. A 1909 study in Cincinnati found some two thousand boys ages ten to thirteen licensed to sell newspapers in the streets, a number that represented about 15 percent of all the boys that age in the city.[29] In many cities newsboys came together in clubhouses or lodgings where for a few cents they could have a cot for the night.

Many of these lodging houses were more than simple shelters and offered the newsboys a variety of ways to better their lives, all structured more or less after the pattern set by Charles Loring Brace. Classes and lectures were held in the lodging houses. They had their own savings banks to encourage thrift, their own courts to settle disputes, and some newsboys' associations published their own monthly newspapers. Unless they were in the South, newsboys' lodging houses generally sheltered a mixture of races and ethnicities.

For much of the nineteenth century newsboys were often homeless and many of them never darkened a school doorway. They got by as best they could, and it was a full-time job to do so. This changed in the twentieth century when child-labor reforms eventually prohibited young children from selling papers in the streets. The second pillar of Brace's ministry to poor and homeless children was shipping them by rail from Manhattan's streets to faraway places where they would be put to work. The first so-called orphan train left Manhattan in 1854 and the program lasted until 1929. By then some 120,000 New York City children had been shipped west.[30]

The orphan trains updated the concept of boarding out. In the colonial era the practice of taking children from their families and putting them out to board and labor in a strange family was strictly local. We can imagine that in colonial villages and towns children placed out with families not their own might occasionally cross paths with members of their biological families and be able to follow their fortunes at close hand. Likewise the families could see what was becoming of their children. But by the 1850s the Industrial Age was underway and nothing was more representative and modern than the railroads. Trainloads of homeless children shipped by rail across the country was an idea that fit well with the changing economic imperatives of an expanding nation. The children would be removed from unhealthy and immoral urban slum surroundings and shipped westward to work and thrive in cleaner air—which meshed nicely with the constant demand for labor in the midwestern states.

Trains might deliver thirty or forty orphans at a time to county seats of these states, where the children would be put on a platform or a stage. Local citizens would choose a child to take home and sign a contract with whatever representative of the Children's Aid Society was accompanying them. In the contract the host would guarantee the child's care. It was a nineteenth-century reworking of the seventeenth-century *vendue*.

One such event involving a shipment of sixteen boys was reported in Mitchell County, Kansas, by the *Cawker City Public Record* in an item from its April 8, 1886, edition. Its description of the event reads little different than if it were describing the scene of a colonial *vendue*, an auctioning of a child's care to the lowest bidder, more than two hundred years earlier: "One of the most interesting events that has recently occurred in Cawker was the distribution of boys from New York City last Saturday.... They were an intelligent lot of little fellows and neatly clad.... All but two can read and write, one of the exceptions being between three and four years old, the ages of the party ranging up to seventeen years."[31]

Charles Loring Brace argued that taking children off the streets and sending them far away to a place where their labor was needed was a win-win solution in which communities benefited on both ends of the process. Potential trouble-makers would be removed from city streets, and towns starved for cheap labor would be supplied. However, the policy's results were not always so beneficial from the point of view of the child in question. Many times the chemistry between the child and his or her receiving family *did* work well, and city kids grew into adults who were upstanding members of small communities—productive, satisfied citizens. In other cases, when the receiving families turned out to be mean, miserly, or abusive or the child recalcitrant, rebellious, or lazy, things did not work out so well.

As was the case with newsboys' lodging houses, the orphan train policy was taken up across the country by nonprofit charitable organizations that cared for homeless children. The Children's Home Society of Chicago, which placed out over three thousand children in the 1890s, published newspaper ads like this one describing a two-year-old boy the society was offering: "Very promising, fine looking, healthy American." In addition the boy came with a money-back guarantee and ninety-day trial period, during which the society would pay the return train fare if a placement did not work out.[32]

Brace stressed that an important factor in determining the success of a placement was eliminating all contact with a child's past life and family. A child's best and perhaps only chance to escape a life of poverty and vice was to give up all connections with the world into which he or she was born. Brace wrote: "The children see nothing but examples of drunkenness, lust, and they grow up inevitably as sharpers, beggers, thieves, burglars, and prostitutes. Amid such communities of outcasts the institutions of education and religion are comparatively powerless."[33]

Even with their constant activity the orphan trains did not make much of a dent in the nation's population of homeless or marginally housed children. The kids placed out by the CAS over the course of seventy years were a small fraction of the children who were growing up homeless or in orphan asylums. Many other desperately poor children did not go anywhere except to work at twelve hours of drudgery for very small wages, which they brought right home. It was not until 1918 that all of the states in the Union had compulsory school attendance laws. Even then the length of time a child was required to stay in school and the degree to which the law was enforced varied substantially from state to state.

.   .   .

Almost a hundred years later in our own day, when school attendance was closely monitored and strictly enforced, homeless families still faced unique problems in making sure that their children were in school every day. When families were uprooted and constantly moving, when no one knew in the morning exactly where they would be sleeping that night, kids just might not be able to get to school some days, Kathi Sheffel told me. It was her job in Fairfax County to see that happened as infrequently as possible. An auburn-haired, solid, middle-aged white woman, she had been the McKinney-Vento liaison for Fairfax County's public schools since 2000.

"When a family loses their housing, kids can transfer schools immediately," she told me. "We try to keep that continuity of going to school in their lives, even if their housing is uncertain.

All that a parent or a school needs to do is contact us. It can take a couple of days to work out the transportation, but we'll keep those kids in school. In class, they're just like their classmates. You've got homeless kids living at a hotel sitting next to kids with parents making lots of money at important jobs in Washington. At school, they're all the same. But what people don't realize is the burden that many of these homeless kids have to carry. They may not know what's going to happen when they leave the building at the end of the school day. They're worried about where they'll sleep, how they'll eat, whether their dad is okay, whether their mom is okay. It's very stressful."[34]

When I interviewed her at her Fairfax office in May 2009, she was coming back from a morning meeting. "I was meeting with a family of six people sleeping on the floor in a small apartment belonging to a disabled relative. One daughter has an important exam coming up today. She was ready and eager to take it. She had been studying, and was confident. That's pretty amazing."

At the time I spoke with her, Kathi Sheffel said she had 1,800 homeless students in the public school system. It was a record high and she said the number had gone up every year since she took the job in 2000. "We're meeting with families all the time. It can be slow going when a family has multiple issues like financial, medical, mental health, disability, job, and housing loss. Sometimes you find all of those at one time. Our number-one priority is keeping kids in school. If they want to go to their old school, they can stay there and we'll arrange transportation. We have over three hundred kids in special transportation right now to keep them in the schools they were attending before their families lost their housing."

A lot of people in Fairfax County lost their homes during the economic recession that struck in 2008, but as in the rest of the

United States Fairfax had a lot of homeless families even before the economy collapsed. When times were good and most people were prospering, the number of people at the bottom, who weren't able to manage, just kept growing. By 2007 monthly rent for a one-bedroom apartment in Fairfax averaged more than $1,200. A little bad luck was all it took to put a family out on the street.

The kind of bad luck for instance that struck Tiffany Wilson* and her family in 2005 when lots of their neighbors were doing just fine. Both she and her husband had good jobs, she told me, but he needed surgeries on his neck and back and could not keep working. Suddenly the income from her job as an office administrator was all they had. They were having a hard time keeping up their Fairfax house payments and then she lost her job because her boss said she took too much time off to deal with her husband's surgeries and care for her children. Shortly thereafter they were living in their car—husband, wife, two teenage boys, and a toddler.

Tiffany Wilson called FACETS and the nonprofit found her a room and a half at the Anchorage and helped pay what it took to keep her there for the next four months. Desperate for work, she took a job as a waitress in a nearby restaurant, making eight dollars an hour. "I'd worked my whole adult life, and never made that little money before," she told me, laughing ruefully. "But I took what was there at that moment. Then I got a file clerk job through a temp agency, and my boss liked how I worked, and now I'm the head of a branch office and I'm making $49,000 a year. I'm renting a townhouse, and in a couple of years I hope to be buying my own house."[35]

When I met her in 2009 she was poised and coiffed, a thirty-eight-year-old African American who remembered those homeless four months as having been harder on her and her marriage (which eventually dissolved) than on her children. "The first three weeks we were at the Anchorage, I cried every day, but my kids never complained. Then I realized I had to make the best of it, and I went and got a waitress job at the first place they said they'd hire me.

"I'm a very hands-on parent. I got a hot plate so I could cook something for my kids, because even though the meals off the meal trucks that came around were okay, they weren't the same thing as their mom's cooking. When we moved into the Anchorage I told the kids, 'This is just something we've got to do to get further,' and all those months they didn't complain once. Not once."

In 2005 Fairfax County had 1,458 homeless people, according to its first point-in-time count, of which an estimated two-thirds were in families. By 2008 the number had jumped to over 1,835 people and county officials recognized the need to act. They drew up a ten-year plan and created an agency, the Office to Prevent and End Homelessness (OPEH), to carry it out. The plan declared: "This commitment requires that no later than December 31, 2018, every person who is homeless or at-risk of being homeless in the Fairfax-Falls Church community will be able to access appropriate affordable housing and the services needed to keep them in their homes."

On January 28, 2009, a point-in-time count found 315 homeless families in Fairfax County, comprising 438 adults and 629 children. Three-quarters of the kids were under twelve years old. Families crowded in with relatives or paying to stay in motels were not counted, putting the actual number of people in homeless families considerably higher. I met with Dean Klein in the spring of 2009 shortly after he took office as the first director of OPEH. Despite the size of the problem he was optimistic.

He told me that OPEH's strategy would consist of two basic components. The first was to standardize the intake screening process and to coordinate and manage all of the services available in the county for the homeless, including homelessness prevention, housing and emergency housing placement, and support services. Up until then a number of different organizations, including the county, nonprofit groups like FACETS, and religious organizations, had worked separately with the homeless.

"Our service delivery system is pretty good; it's a pretty well-established system in the county. We have a lot of providers who have been doing good work for a long time. What we're doing now is kind of a new way of operating, including the process, the partnership, and a more focused way of ending homelessness rather than serving homelessness. We're looking at more creative ways of dealing with the problem. Many of these programs are focused in the right direction, but now with the ten-year plan we're poised to make adjustments to where the priority in dollars and resources are."[36]

The second part of OPEH's strategy was to develop a capacity for the rapid rehousing of homeless families. The county had just been awarded a three-year, $2.46 million grant in "stimulus" funding from the federal Homelessness Prevention and Rapid Rehousing Program. OPEH would use much of it as rental assistance in a "housing first" strategy integral to the plan for ending homelessness, Klein told me in 2009. For instance a family that was living in a motel would not move to a shelter when a space became available, and then on to housing, but instead would go directly into housing and then utilize the support services necessary to stay housed.

"One of the principles of 'housing first' is rapid rehousing. What has been happening is a family would go from a motel to a shelter and staying there, and receiving comprehensive services there, and then they had to be moved into housing. The premise of 'housing first' is that you are more rapidly moving the family into housing, then providing the services to them in the community, because there's more likelihood that they'll then become self-sufficient there. With our families that are staying in motels, what we're hoping to do is prevent them from entering into the shelter by identifying housing opportunities so that, in fact, we can provide the services to them in housing rather than entering the shelter system. We'll be using the stimulus dollars to provide rental assistance from three to eighteen months.

"One of the key elements of 'housing first' is prevention. You can serve people on the back end, but until you start to stem the flow of people coming into homelessness it's hard to affect the numbers. I would expect this will be reflected in a reduced waiting list for shelter space over the coming years. We have sought national best practices, for example, by bringing in the National Alliance to End Homelessness who have helped to really develop the concept of 'housing first.' They've worked with over three hundred communities nationally.

"Take, for instance, people who have wound up in a motel room because they've lost their jobs. The groups working with the families in motels will direct them toward the rental subsidies. By providing them with the rental assistance and connecting them with the support services, we can stabilize them. The stimulus dollars are going to be available for two to three years, so at some point there'll have to be an increased commitment from the county, if that's working."

. . .

In 2009 many Virginia license plates bore the motto "Kids First." This public concern for the state's children was a little hard to take seriously at the Anchorage Motel on any early weekday morning when half a dozen homeless kids were waiting for the school bus. If it was raining or snowing, they gathered in the lobby and kept watch through the big, plateglass window. The Anchorage had been a regular school bus stop since 1997. The drivers ran the route so that the children were the first to be picked up and the last to be dropped off; this way their classmates would not know they were living in a motel.

On any given morning the children waiting for the school bus were of different races, nationalities, and religions. The narratives of their parents' hard luck that brought them to the Anchorage took many different forms, but these kids had some things in common. They were at risk of being in poorer health than their housed classmates, and the chances were greater that their lives would be marked by violence or substance abuse. Still, as I looked at them gathered by the window, they seemed to shine like any other kids, generally enthusiastic and excited, glad to be alive.

Talia Abouela*'s daughters—eleven-year-old Grace* and ten-year-old Hiba*—were among them. Talia wound up at the Anchorage because she could not abide any more physical abuse from a man. She was a single mother who had left her home in Khartoum, Sudan, with her two girls eight years before to join her sister in Houston, Texas. The father of her two daughters stayed behind.

In Texas she obtained a green card and settled in. She met and married another Sudanese refugee in Houston with whom she had a son, Kamal*, she told me in a mix of English and Arabic translated by eleven-year-old Grace. The man drank and he beat her and the girls, she said, her daughters nodding assent. In the spring of 2009 she made the decision to leave him and go to Fairfax, Virginia. For a brief time she crowded into an apartment with a Sudanese family she had met in Texas who had told her about Fairfax, where they lived. Then she quickly got on the public assistance rolls and applied for a place in a public shelter.[37]

She was put on the waiting list and her case was passed to FACETS. The nonprofit was paying for her stay at the Anchorage. Talia Abouela had been at the motel for a month when I met her. She was seven months pregnant. Talia's belly bulged beneath the colorful shawls that she wore wrapped around her in layers, made of the same gauzy material as the scarf that always covered her head when she padded up and down the sidewalk along the row of one-story, brick motel rooms, shod in thin flip-flops, a hand on her hip, moving with the rolling gait of advanced pregnancy. During the day she and four-year-old Kamal were alone in the motel room while the girls were at school. The television was always on. Talia seemed to be in a permanently semi-dazed state, the only certainty in her life being the pending birth.

Every evening at six the church volunteers in the FACETS program made their stop at the Anchorage and distributed the meals they had prepared. When motel residents heard the distinctive three-note honk, they came out of their rooms and lined up to receive as many hot meals in Styrofoam containers as they needed for their families. In addition to Grace, her mother, and siblings, in the line of some thirty people at the Anchorage each night were people who hailed from many different parts of the globe. It was a United Nations of people down on their luck waiting for supper.

Talia was grateful for the church meals because otherwise she acknowledged that her family might not have eaten some evenings. But the food was tasteless and bland to her palate and she longed for foods that pleased her. She eagerly accepted my offer of a ride for herself and the three kids to the nearest supermarket where they spent $90 in food stamps on things that did not need more cooking than a motel microwave could accomplish. Talia pulled a box of fish sticks out of the freezer at the supermarket and passed it to Grace. "Ready?" she asked, meaning is it microwave-ready?

Grace read the instructions on the box, which her mother's English was not sufficient to do, and shook her head. Her mother frowned in disappointment and put it back in the freezer. She pulled out another brand of frozen fish sticks from the shelf below and Grace read it, then explained to her mother that they all said the same thing. None of the boxes of fish sticks were microwave-able. The only fish they could get with the food stamps were some cans of tuna. "All I want is a room that has somewhere I can cook," Talia said.

Grace told me that her younger sister Hiba's school performance had declined since moving to the Anchorage, while hers had held its own. I was not surprised about that. She was a smart girl who shut out the world with a book and spent a lot of time on the sole, old, slow desktop computer in the Anchorage's lobby, paying absolutely no attention to whatever else was going on there.

"What we're studying in school that's really interesting is how the body changes," Grace told me, as I pushed a grocery cart down the cereal aisle and she followed alongside, picking out first one box then a second. "How puberty affects you. Girls go through it first, you know. A girl can get pregnant after it happens so she must be careful who she associates with, and how she behaves."

"Hm, that's right," I said, more than a little surprised by the turn the conversation had taken. My discomfort amused her. Grace did not smile a lot but when she did her face illuminated. She was three years old when they moved from Khartoum to

Houston. She and her sister had been educated as Americans. Her unaccented English was flawless and she was well spoken. Grace missed Houston, her friends, and the apartment where they had lived. Her mother told me through Grace that she missed it too, because it had a kitchen.

·   ·   ·

By 2014, five years after I first spoke with Dean Klein, substantial progress had been made in Fairfax, although the county was still not near the 2018 goal of ending family homelessness. Between 2005 and 2008 the numbers of people in homeless families had risen from 933 to 1,091. In 2009 OPEH was formed and since then the numbers had gone steadily down. In January 2014 the point-in-time survey counted 695 homeless people in families, well below the 2005 level.[38]

Klein was still OPEH's director in 2014, and while he agreed that the county remained a long way from ending family homelessness he was encouraged by the latest figures and he was optimistic that by 2018 no head of family in Fairfax County would be homeless against her or his will. The federal stimulus funding that jump-started OPEH only lasted through 2011, but Klein and his agency were able to use it and prove to local officials that the numbers of homeless families could be substantially reduced. When the stimulus money ran out, Fairfax County picked up the slack, he told me when we spoke in May 2014. In addition the county had put a central resource number in place, a one-call hub from which people were referred to OPEH or other appropriate services.

"Since 2009, we've enhanced our prevention efforts tremendously. We're keeping people in their homes a lot more effectively, so that they don't have to become homeless to get housing.

What we did was identify stimulus dollars, and then local dollars, for rental subsidies to keep people in their homes rather than entering homelessness. We're helping them deal with debt; we're working with domestic violence problems and other issues that impact their ability to remain in stable housing. We had ninety families in motels at one point. Now it's down to two. We now have a system and policies that reflect priorities—where you're going to allocate resources in a smart way. To the extent possible we're prioritizing keeping people in their homes; to the extent possible we're valuing the fact that motels are not a safe place.

"And to the extent possible we're using the county resources for shelter in a more effective way so that people who are in the shelters really need to be in shelters because of more elaborate needs, and that those who we can prevent, we do. On the back end, when someone becomes homeless, we're a lot more aggressive and effective at moving people into permanent housing. The average length of time of stay in shelters in 2009 was three months. Then we designed our intake system and now it's three to five days. We don't have a waiting list for shelters anymore."[39]

Klein stressed that many times it was not enough simply to move someone out of a shelter and into vacant housing. "There's a case plan developed on any entrance into shelter. We know that with a shorter length of stay, it requires more and more targeting of priorities of how you spend your time with them, and what you're prioritizing. Certainly housing is one, but also employment and other factors like that, so when they move out they have a greater chance of being successful."

The OPEH program was highlighted in the April 2011 monthly report from the National Alliance to End Homelessness (NAEH). "Ending homelessness is absolutely the correct goal for Fairfax County and for the nation," Nan Roman, president of the NAEH, told the *Washington Post.* "To be clear, ending homelessness does not mean that people won't continue to have housing crises and lose their housing. What it does mean is that when they do, the crisis will be quickly resolved and they will not be spending months or years living in a shelter."[40]

Dean Klein was certain OPEH was on the right track. "We've been hugely successful with our housing-first approach, and accelerating our success with moving people out of homelessness and into permanent housing. Eighty-nine percent of the families that exited shelter in 2011 had not returned to homelessness after two years." Since the first time I had spoken with him in 2009, Klein had become increasingly convinced that the basic problem underlying family homelessness is not a shiftless, substance-abusing head of family, nor any personal failings on the part of the poor, but simply a lack of affordable housing. One of the things Klein began urging Fairfax County to do when working with homeless families was to fill vacant social worker and case manager positions with people who understood real estate, who were landlords, or had a real estate license. "We were able to encourage nonprofits and county agencies to change the social work positions that had been filled by social workers to housing locators," he told me in 2014. "What that meant was that we encouraged them to recognize what was happening.

"At the time we made that shift and they began to retool those positions, the social work positions were not being filled by people with real estate or housing backgrounds; when a vacancy occurred people were being hired who had a social work background. People who understand real estate can more successfully establish relationships with landlords, better understand the market, better understand how to work with people on leases and arrears, and other issues that faced people who were home-less, and they could move people more rapidly out of shelters and into housing. That was a huge effort. There's never enough housing, but what you'll find is that the number of people exiting emergency shelter for permanent housing in 2011 was 280 fami-lies, and in 2013 it was 561 families.

"A housing locator network was created. We put out an RFP [request for proposal], and we have a nonprofit that operates this under contract. We started with federal stimulus dollars, saw the success of it, and were able to locate local dollars from Fairfax County. Ninety-seven percent of the families housed through the housing locator network remain in permanent housing one year later." Most families, he said, fall into homelessness because they cannot pay market-value rents even when the breadwinner holds a job or two. With enough places to live that were afforda-ble for someone trying to support a family on a minimum wage, Klein was convinced that homelessness in Fairfax County would virtually disappear.

Patrick Markee, a senior policy analyst with New York City's Coalition for the Homeless, agreed with him and said the same thing was true in the city's five boroughs. He had been working with homeless families in the city for twenty years, and he pointed to New York's astronomical rents as the primary cause of the growing population of homeless families. "I think you could eliminate virtually all family homelessness if you had suf-ficient affordable housing resources," Markee, who is also a board member of the National Coalition for the Homeless, told me in May 2014. "Our research and experience over the years kind of supports that.

"Homelessness, at its root, is an affordability problem. The families we work with are working-poor families, or unemployed families. A lot of them do have other service needs, dealing with issues of substance abuse or domestic violence; they or their kids may have physical health problems. But these problems are not the reasons they're homeless. They're homeless because they cannot afford to pay rent."[41]

New York was the only place in the United States besides Washington, DC, and the Commonwealth of Massachusetts with a law mandating that shelter had to be provided for eligible homeless families. About 18 percent of the nation's 222,000 people in homeless families on the night of 2013's point-in-time count were in New York City.[42] Anything that worked to reduce family homelessness in New York would mean an important reduction in national numbers.

In 2013 many cities across the country had record numbers of families in need of emergency shelter, and New York was among them. More than twenty thousand homeless children were in New York City's shelters on any given night in 2013, an all-time high according to the Coalition for the Homeless's annual report.[43] Over a billion dollars was spent in 2014 providing shelter and services to homeless individuals and families, according to Markee.

The number of homeless children in the city increased by 8 percent over the course of 2013, reaching all-time highs each month. Not only were more children in the city's shelters, but the average stay for a homeless family was 14.5 months (435 days), the longest ever recorded. By the end of 2014 one in every forty-three kids in New York had slept in a city shelter during the year. Fifty-seven percent of the children in city shelters were African Americans and 30.8 percent were Latinos.[44]

The quality of care in those shelters can be judged by the fact that in early 2014, even with the city's shelters full to capacity, four hundred children and their families were removed from two of them, which were judged unfit for minors. The *New York Times* reported, "For nearly three decades, thousands of children passed through Auburn and Catherine Street, living with cockroaches, spoiled food, violence and insufficient heat, even as inspectors warned that the shelters were unfit for children."[45]

Michael Bloomberg, the billionaire mayor of New York City from 2003 through 2013, oversaw a rise in numbers of homeless families to record high levels. Many observers have concluded that his policies exacerbated the problem. At the end of Bloomberg's tenure three distinct kinds of shelters for homeless families with children existed in New York City. The first model was the standard shelter run by a nonprofit organization; the second was welfare hotels and motels; and the third was a building with empty apartments in it.

"This model uses empty apartments as shelters and paying the landlords ridiculous amounts of money, three thousand dollars a month," said Patrick Markee. "Nine years ago, the city stopped taking any federal rental vouchers and created these really badly designed short-term subsidy programs. The subsidy would get cut off after a year or two and they'd be back in shelters. We've had two mayors, Giuliani and Bloomberg, with a view of the world that if you take away housing resources there'll be fewer homeless people; if you treat people badly and put a lot of punitive rules in place, make people's lives miserable, they'll go away. They won't. They didn't."

Nevertheless he was hopeful, impressed by the new mayor, Bill de Blasio, and his commitment to battling family homelessness. De Blasio's program, announced shortly after he took office, called for 200,000 units of affordable housing to be made available over ten years. Things looked grim during de Blasio's first year in office as the number of homeless families continued to rise, even while the new mayor began putting programs into effect. Month after month in 2014 the tally rose—by 132 in February, 206 in May, more than 300 over summer, and 800 or so in the fall—so that by the end of his first year in office the mayor had presided over a 14 percent increase in the shelter census of families with children. But in the early months of 2015 the number of homeless families began to drop and advocates for homeless families were hopeful that the programs were gaining traction.

If so it was a long time coming, according to Markee. "This has been the worst period of family homelessness in the city's history. We need to move at least 5,000 families a year into subsidized housing. If we move 7,500 families a year, we would see a two-thirds reduction within five years. That would work for most people. Families don't want to be on the streets; they want to be in their own homes. The reason they are on the streets is because they don't want to be in shelters—a lot of shelters are crappy shelters—but they do want to have a lock and a key, and a door and their own home, and if you can provide them services to help them maintain stability and get healthy, all the better. I believe you could move most homeless families out of shelter and into housing today, and they'd do quite well."

This is not a unanimous opinion among people who work with homeless families. In New York City, for instance, the housing readiness model still has its advocates who hold that simply rehousing a family as rapidly as possible is not enough. Stabilize them first in a shelter, or transitional housing, and prepare them with skills that will help them not just find a place to live but that will enable them to stay housed. Proponents of this model generally see housing first/rapid rehousing as a way to minimize the amount of money spent on housing homeless families, and a smoke screen behind which more expensive and time-consuming strategies are eliminated, even though they are eventually a surer path to housing stability.

The Institute for Children, Poverty and Homelessness (ICPH) has worked with homeless families in New York City since 1990 and is affiliated with a nonprofit, Homes for the Homeless (HFH), founded in 1986 by Leonard Stern of the Hartz Corporation in cooperation with St. John the Divine Cathedral and city government. In 2015 HFH administered three family shelters around greater New York City. At any given time the three had a total capacity to house 431 homeless families with approximately 625 children. The HFH website explained:

> Rather than assume parents will have the opportunity to obtain services once they have procured permanent housing, HFH ensures that a family's future can begin as soon as they walk through the doors....
>
> Each [shelter] provides a community of opportunity where families find the classrooms, libraries, computer labs, health clinics, playgrounds, and counseling centers they will use during their time as residents. All of these on-site resources make a place where parents and children can learn and grow as they embark on the path to independence. Mothers drop toddlers off at daycare on their way to work, after-school teachers greet kids as they come home from school, and families learn together in literacy workshops. While students take educational field trips to museums and city landmarks, adults meet with employment and housing specialists who help them prepare for job interviews and find apartments of their own.[46]

In an April 2013 report Ralph da Costa Nunez, a Columbia University faculty member at the School of International and Public Affairs, and CEO of the ICPH, wrote that the high recidivism rate of families returning to shelters who had received

Bloomberg-era rental subsidies proved that housing-first strategies are not a panacea for family homelessness: "The lesson to be
drawn from all of this should be clear: 'one size fits all' policies
for addressing family homelessness do not work. Not all families
are equal. Some families successfully transitioned to permanent
housing after their shelter stays, but others did not. Rapid
Rehousing was a failed experiment that produced unwanted
incentives and unwarranted costs." [47]

·   ·   ·

Back in 2009 at the Anchorage, Talia Abouela told me, using her
daughter Grace to translate, that she and her three children
were resigned to the fact that she would be giving birth before
they would be able to leave the motel. The room where the four
of them lived had a bathroom and one room with two double
beds—mother and four-year-old Kamal in one, the two girls in
the other; a bar-sized refrigerator in a corner; a long motel
bureau with a mirror on the wall behind it. On top of the bureau
were a microwave and a large television. Soon a newborn baby
would be joining them. It would be hard, Grace told me in 2009,
the last time I spoke with her, but they would get by. "I just want
to be living somewhere normal again," she said, an undertone of
longing in her voice. "That's all. Just somewhere normal."

CHAPTER FOUR

Portland, Oregon

The Modern Almshouse

There are few things more vital to the welfare of the
nation than accurate and dependable knowledge of the
best methods of dealing with children, especially with
those who are in one way or another handicapped by
misfortune; and in the absence of such knowledge
each community is left to work out its own problem
without being able to learn of and profit by the success
or failure of other communities along the same lines
of endeavor.[1]

Theodore Roosevelt, February 1909

The Pacific Northwest had a substantial population of transients
for much of the twentieth century, people who were on the
move through Idaho, Washington, Oregon, and Northern California. They harvested seasonal crops or worked in logging
camps in an era when the cutting and transporting of the Northwest's vast timber resources required largely manual labor.
They were people who for whatever reasons, economic or otherwise, had abandoned aspirations to stable lives in one place
with jobs and families. They rode the rails, worked, did or did

not send money home, did or did not have a home to send it to. Many of these people lived part of the year in Portland.

Transients came to reside for a while in one of the city's single-room occupancy (SRO) hotels mostly in the district called Burnside close to the Willamette River—hotels with rates almost anyone could afford in a neighborhood with a long-established network of cheap bars and restaurants that served filling food and strong drink at reasonably low prices. In 1976 a local census counted twenty-six SROs in Portland. [2] Many of these hotels had lobbies with comfortable old chairs grouped around big console televisions. Even without such amenities the rooms provided shelter from wet, cold winter weather, a warm place to pass out when drunk, and a door to lock before doing so. In the seasons when work was available people often labored just long enough to accumulate what was needed to live weeks or months on Skid Row (named after the old wooden roads built to slide logs into a river). When they needed money they'd go back to work. Paid labor was not hard to find: during seasonal crop harvests as many as fifty farm buses would be waiting on the streets of a morning to transport anyone who wanted a day's work to the fields, bringing them back in the evening.[3]

The transients—most often men but with some women counted among them—frequently overwintered in Portland. When the temperatures began to drop a migration toward the city got under way among people from around the Northwest. Hobos, tramps, and transients began to make preparations for the coming winter. Often that meant roosting in an SRO hotel, spending the wages saved over the rest of the year on a cheap room and months of drinking, catching up with old friends, and making new ones.

Burnside's population was by no means restricted to transients. The Chinese first settled there in the mid-nineteenth century, opening groceries, laundries, and cheap hotels for Chinese migrant workers. The district, always a little sinister and mysterious, was said to be honeycombed by tunnels beneath the streets, originally constructed for drainage. Tales were told of men on a Portland drunk who were shanghaied: drugs slipped into their drinks, they were carried to the Willamette River through the tunnels, waking to find themselves as crew on ships that had weighed anchor and were headed down the Columbia River toward the Pacific Ocean and on to Asia.

A number of excellent Chinese restaurants with tables in booths behind curtains opened in the early twentieth century, and they were patronized by Chinese and white Portlanders alike. People came from all over the city to dine in those secluded booths—businessmen to make deals and couples to enjoy the privacy. After the Chinese came waves of Greek and Japanese immigration adding to the Burnside district's ethnic and cultural mix.

Through it all the transients remained as a constant population. Day centers with names like Baloney Joe's and Sisters of the Road served men and women, along with the bars and hotels. In the mid-1970s, a weekly street newspaper appeared—at first called *The Hobo News* and later *The BCC Pipeline*—carrying news of local goings-on like the annual parade when a hobo king and queen were crowned.

By the winter of 2014 things had changed dramatically. Many of those Burnside district properties were no longer serving transients. No more than a dozen SRO hotels remained in the entire city, and their numbers continued to shrink as developers turned them into office buildings, condominiums, and upscale watering holes. Portland had become an attractive place to live for young professionals despite the fact that it had an inordinate number of cold, rainy, gray days. It offered a tolerant, environmentally aware, alternative community made up of many people trying to live sustainable urban lives. Bicycle traffic was prodigious and it seemed as if half the Volkswagen vans still running in North America were in Portland.

The sorts of people who were on the streets of the Burnside district fifty years before had virtually disappeared. Those who wandered the district during the winter of 2014 were an entirely different breed. They were not relaxing after a few months of work. Wrapped in many layers of clothes, they were chronically homeless individuals, all their belongings with them in packs on their backs, or garbage bags over their shoulders, or grocery carts skittering along the sidewalk in front of them. They slept under bridges or beneath overpasses, or in camps down by the river.

Most of these people would not be leaving to look for work in the spring, nor at any other time in the near future. Many were mentally ill and incapable of finding a job or housing. Others had substance abuse problems and the substance they abused was all too often methamphetamine. The only job open to many of them was devoting a few hours a day to selling copies of *Street Roots,* the weekly "homeless newspaper" published since 1998—a successor of a sort to *The BCC Pipeline.* Most vendors of *Street Roots* would not make much more money selling the paper than just enough to buy something to eat with a little left over.

The city's climate brought its own problems for the chronically homeless. "In Portland, it doesn't get so cold in the winter that you can't survive, but what happens is that it's so rainy and so wet, that you're damp all the time," said Israel Bayer, the thirty-eight-year-old editor of *Street Roots.* "It creates both a physical and psychological situation that's very wearing. It's not unusual to have high levels of the flu, or walking pneumonia. Over the course of a winter, it takes a toll."[4]

Since Bayer arrived in Portland in 1997, he had seen the Burnside district go through both boom and bust economies, he told me in the fall of 2014. "Right now, Portland is experiencing an economic boom. The rental market is all over the place. When the recession hit, a whole lot of families that were only a paycheck or two away from being homeless fell into it. We've seen many more families in this situation. A lot of breaking up of families, because you may be able to find a place for a woman and a young child with the family safety net, or doubled up in housing, but the men in the families are staying out on the streets, selling *Street Roots*."

Through all the city's economic cycles Portland's population of homeless families had followed the national trend and risen steadily since the mid-1980s. Before then and despite the large transient population, homeless families with children were virtually unknown. That had changed: in the 2013–14 school year officials counted 1,367 homeless students in public schools and preschools, including 99 who were under the age of two.[5] Among the literally homeless population, which included unsheltered families plus those in emergency shelter, the number of persons in families with children increased by seventy-two individuals, or 18 percent, between 2011 and 2013. The point-in-time count for the city in 2013 identified 474 families with children who were unsheltered or in emergency shelter,[6] and some observers believed an equal number of families had gone uncounted.

Families living doubled up don't get counted, but a student living in such a situation is in fact a homeless child, said Portland Public Schools' Title X administrator Marti Heard. "There's just a huge discrepancy between the shelter space and housing that we need, and what's available. It's staggering. Our largest group of homeless students are those who are doubled up, their families are living with friends or relatives."

Portland presented a strange contrast: the sidewalks of the riverfront Burnside district were teeming with the chronically homeless surrounded by the city's numerous hip, environmentally friendly neighborhoods, each in the midst of a real estate boom. Between 2000 and 2013 the city had the second-fastest-growing economy in the country. The top one percent of the city's wage earners saw their incomes reach record levels,[7] but the rising tide did not lift all boats as evidenced by a growing number of homeless families over that same period.

. . .

The United States has seen the gap between its richest and poorest residents widen during other cycles of its history. The years between 1875 and 1909 were an economic era of growing affluence for the well-to-do and hard times for the poor, many of whom were trying to raise children without the means to keep a roof over their heads. Child reformers exerted increasing political pressure on Washington. The situation became too drastic to ignore.

In 1909 President Theodore Roosevelt declared that the care of dependent children must be a national priority and that he was ready to do whatever it took to address the problem. He convened the country's leading experts to a conference at the White House to design a policy. The invitation read in part, "Surely nothing ought to interest our people more than the cause of the children who are destitute and neglected but not delinquent."

The 1909 White House Conference on the Care of Dependent Children marked the first time in the history of the nation that the federal government recognized it had some responsibility for such children. The decision to become involved in dealing with destitute families brought an end to centuries when the central government entirely turned its back on the poorest of its children by leaving states and municipalities to shoulder the financial burden of keeping them fed and housed. The Gilded Age was beginning to transform into the Progressive Era.

An increasing public awareness and the growing political clout of the child savers' movement had brought the situation of the nation's desperately poor children to the forefront of Roosevelt's agenda. The participants in the 1909 White House Conference presented their conclusions to the president after two days of meetings. Their report left no room for doubt as to how they felt about congregate emergency shelter: "The sending of children of any age or class to almshouses is an unqualified evil, and should be forbidden everywhere by law, with suitable penalty for its violation."

The conference's final report included nine proposals. One of them was a recommendation for the founding of a national foster care program. Theodore Roosevelt had made his support for foster care abundantly clear: "Personally, I very earnestly believe that the best way in which to care for dependent children is in the family home. In Massachusetts, many orphan asylums have been discontinued and thousands of the children who formally have gone to the orphan asylum are now kept in private homes."[8]

Foster care was hardly a new concept in public policy. Historians point to nine-year-old Benjamin Eaton as the New World's first foster child—indentured for fourteen years to Bridget Fuller by order of the Plymouth governor in 1636. Benjamin's parents had both arrived on the *Mayflower* and between them they had twelve children and little income. They lived in straitened circumstances and by 1643 they had been ordered to place four more children with other families. The couple's daughter Elizabeth was six years old when she was put out to work in another family's household, and her younger brother, Joseph, was apprenticed when he was only five.[9]

Who knows how many hundreds of thousands or even millions of poor children followed them over the next two hundred years—placed out, indentured, apprenticed—to grow up in an equivalent of foster care's roll of the dice. They were raised in families not their own, dependent on people who were not their parents who took responsibility for them out of compassion or out of avarice, for better or for worse.

By 1909 the practices of indenture, apprenticeship, and placing out had virtually disappeared and the need for a formal foster care system was evident. Over the course of the twentieth century the federal government took an increasingly active role in legislating and financing foster care, which became the primary policy tool for dealing with dependent and neglected children. In 1910, 61,000 children were estimated to be in foster care and in 1960 the number was 163,000;[10] by 2014 that number was up to 415,129 children in foster care on a given night,[11] and the annual federal budget called for almost $4.3 billion to cover foster care maintenance and administrative costs. Over the twentieth century the federal government had taken over the role of primary care funder for the children of those who could not do for themselves.

. . .

In Portland when the heads of families who were homeless or were in danger of losing their shelter began to look for public assistance, their first step was to call 211, Portland's central helpline. Callers were screened on the phone and ranked on a vulnerability index. If it was determined that they met the definition of homeless, they were put on a waiting list to see a "mobile housing specialist," Troy Hammond, the director of 211, told me in the fall of 2014.

A mobile housing specialist's job was to make an in-depth evaluation of families, determine how they could best find housing, and find what funds if any were available to help them do so. Portland had eight such housing specialists, each carrying a caseload of fifteen to thirty families. Some 1,500 officially homeless families—many of them doubled up in barely livable situations—were on a waiting list to receive the services of one of the housing specialists; it could take quite a while to resolve each case, Hammond told me. Among those waiting were more than two hundred families whose situations were deemed absolutely untenable and who were in need of immediate emergency shelter.[12]

The only thing that the county had to offer those families was the Warming Center. Each year from November 1 to May 1 Multnomah County opened a winter shelter where families could come to sleep out of the rain and cold. Despite the cozy name the Warming Center provided nothing more than the most bare-bones congregate housing along with suppers provided by volunteers from local congregations. The winter shelter was administered under contract with the county by Human Solutions, a Portland nonprofit. The contract ran from November through March, and with an extra $30,000 donated by a local business the shelter stayed open a month longer, until the end of April.

The winter shelter never turned a family away and Multnomah County could legitimately claim during the winter months that no waiting list for emergency family shelter existed. If the winter shelter was full a second shelter was opened in a church basement. Human Solutions also maintained a day shelter at a different church, which was a couple of bus rides distant. It offered showers, laundry facilities, and computer terminals.

As a rule the farther one headed east from downtown Portland, the poorer the residents. The Warming Center was in a neighborhood far from downtown with lots of unpaved streets rutted with muddy potholes and small yards with tall Douglas firs towering over modest houses. The winter shelter was in a former Social Security office, which the city had converted into a methadone dispensary until the neighbors forced its closure. The neighborhood's residents were poor but even so they didn't want the methadone clinic in their backyard with its line of people waiting for their daily doses, then hanging around afterward with no place to go. The shelter, on the other hand, didn't open until 7 P.M., long after nightfall during Portland's winter months, and families had to be out by 7 A.M. when it was still dark. Neighbors never saw these families. The shelter constituted one small community in the invisible nation. It was a long way out on the east side of the city, but the light-rail public transport had a stop right in front of the shelter. It cost $2.50 for an adult to make the ride out from the city's center. Kids under five were free and those between five and eighteen paid a discounted fare.

Inside, the building's former incarnation as a government office was still very much in evidence. The Warming Center consisted of a dozen small offices around an open central area. When they arrived families were doubled up in the little office spaces or they slept in the central zone, which was filled with cots. Children or adults were permitted to ask for a black foam-rubber mat on the floor instead of a cot. Supper was served courtesy of local church groups.

The average length of stay at the winter shelter was about forty days according to Jean DeMaster, the executive director of

Human Solutions. I went to see her on November 1, the first night the shelter was open in 2014. Five families showed up to pass a cold, rainy, post-Halloween night: seven adults and eight children. Within a week it would be full every night, DeMaster confidently predicted. In 2013, she said, the winter shelter and its overflow space housed 150 people a night.

Jean DeMaster was a thin, focused, gray-haired white woman who had been the director at Human Solutions since 2002. "I think the situation we're seeing now is pretty dire," she told me. "What we see here is people having very little income, and being unable to afford their housing and being doubled up. Not having enough food for the kids for three meals a day, not having winter jackets now that it's getting cold.[13]

"The first priority is to get people inside, get them into the shelter system so they don't have to stay outside anymore, and their kids aren't in danger. Sometimes you see these little babies that have been staying in cars, and it's freezing cold, you know? It's a little infant. That's just not right." The winter shelter was in place to keep that from happening. But, said DeMaster, the next step was equally important: "Get people out of shelter as quickly as possible, and when possible bypass the shelter system and go right into the housing program. The key to that is housing specialists and rent assistance."

DeMaster said that Human Solutions' experience with rapid rehousing was positive. About 85 percent of the families that moved into housing with rental assistance were still housed a year after the rent subsidies had stopped. "We shifted from housing readiness to rapid rehousing in the late 1990s. It's so much more effective to get families into an apartment as quickly as you can, and get people on the track of being able to pay for that apartment themselves.

"We still offer money management classes, but if you take a money management class and you're living in a shelter, how can you use that information? If you're living in an apartment, and you've been there for a month or two, and you take a money management class, then you're dealing with your actual situation, and the class will make a lot more sense."

Each spring when the winter shelter closed, the city's homeless families were pretty much out of luck as far as municipal assistance went. Portland's various religious congregations organized the year so that each night a different place of worship was opened to serve as a one-night family shelter. Other than that, between May 1 and October 31 only a dozen fixed shelter spaces for homeless families existed in the entire city, administered by two nonprofit agencies. The Goose Hollow shelter had eight of those spaces and was open all year. It was located in the basement gymnasium of a vast church building in southwest Portland's Goose Hollow neighborhood, and the eight spaces it offered were always full. Families slept on mats in cubicles divided by eight curtained partitions on wheels, which folded up along the walls of the gym during the day. Families had to be at the shelter before 6:30 P.M. and back out on the streets at 7:30 A.M. The shelter was managed by a nonprofit, Portland Homeless Family Solutions (PHFS), which also had a day shelter a few blocks away.

Dinner was prepared and served to the eight families at the shelter every night of the year by volunteers from area congregations. The Goose Hollow shelter also relied on volunteers to stay overnight with homeless families. Two volunteers spent each night with the eight families, then set breakfast out for them the next morning before shooing everyone out to the streets at 7:30, rain or shine. It was almost always rain.

The average family spent about forty nights in the shelter until affordable housing was located or until they could no longer bear it and found someone to take them in temporarily, said Matt Kertman, who was Goose Hollow's director of volunteer services in October 2014. Forty days was the average but a much longer stay was not uncommon and families sometimes went as long as 120 nights sleeping on the gym floor. After that they had to leave because state law ruled that anyone in the same place for more than 120 days was in "permanent" housing and could not be asked to leave but must be evicted.

No cots were available at Goose Hollow, only foam rubber mats laid out on the gym floor inside the cubicles. The shiny surfaces of the thick mats all had duct-tape patches. They were "Tempurpedic" foam mats, and fifty of them cost ten thousand dollars according to Kertman, so PHFS patched what they had for as long as they could. The night I volunteered, among the eight families was one that had only spent 19 nights at the shelter and another that had been there for 113 and was fast approaching its 120-night limit.

Two of the eight families were actually members of the same family, a grandmother, mother, and five kids. In the half hour before lights-out, the families sat in folding chairs around aluminum tables. The grandmother cradled her head in her arms on the table, never looking up. The two boys and three girls hovered around her chair, touching her, murmuring in her ear. Later, after the lights were out, she snored loudly, her snoring intermittently interrupted by her loud yelps, exclamations, and recriminations audible throughout the gym while she dreamed.

In the next cubicle over from this family slept Andrea Gould* and her twelve-year-old son Adam*. They were right at the average forty-day stay. She was lithe and muscular and looked ten years younger than her forty-six years, with long blonde hair, strikingly clear blue eyes, and a flower-and-vine tattoo trailing down her right arm. Andrea was articulate and intelligent with an inquiring mind. She had put her dreams of college and a degree on hold after her divorce, earning her paramedic's certification so she could support her three children. She worked nine years as a paramedic, but when she ruptured a disc on the job she began sliding toward homelessness.

"You can't wait for help lifting someone and getting them into an ambulance if they're lying on the floor having a heart attack," she told me. "People are definitely much, much bigger than they used to be. When I started, it was once or twice a month you had someone who weighed over three hundred pounds, but by the time I got hurt it was once or twice a day that me and my partner were lifting someone that heavy onto a gurney."[14]

She said her surgeon botched the disc repair leaving her in constant pain. Her health benefits ran out and she was unable to find a job that did not require lifting or physical labor. "I'm pretty specifically trained in the medical field, and it doesn't really translate to doing another thing. It's a good field to be in, if you can do that type of work. I'm a really good diagnostician, but you still have to be qualified to do the *whole* job, including lifting, or you don't do any of it."

She lost her house. Her two older daughters, twenty-two and eighteen, shared a small apartment in Portland but there was not room for Andrea and Adam. They moved in with a relative. "He made $120,000 a year, and he was constantly complaining about working hard and paying taxes so lazy people like me could live off government handouts. His wife was almost an obsessive-compulsive. Even though I spent hours cleaning, I could never have the house clean enough for her. We had to move out. We couch-surfed for a while, and wound up homeless. I've never been homeless before."

Andrea was raised in a Christian household by her parents but long ago was drawn to Buddhism. She practiced Vipassana meditation every morning at the day shelter before going out to look for housing. "I try to keep a positive outlook. The meditation helps a lot. I don't know how I'd be doing if I didn't have that."

A mobile housing specialist had found some possible sources of rental assistance if Andrea was able to find a cheap vacant unit. Such a find would be only slightly this side of miraculous in Portland with its single-digit vacancy rate in rental housing and a citywide deficit of some twenty-two thousand units of affordable housing.[15] Nevertheless she had already come close to finding a place suitable for her and Adam, and was confident that shortly they would be back in a home of their own.

Andrea was not the only person I met at the Goose Hollow shelter who attributed her or his homelessness to health issues. Some, like Andrea, had physical health problems. One was a white construction worker injured in an accident on the job, who became homeless with his six-year-old son when his workers' comp ran out. Or the health issue was mental, as in the case of a lively, animated, African American mother of a ten-year-old boy. She had awoken the year before in their apartment, sunk in too deep a depression to go to work. She stopped going out almost entirely, lost her job and the apartment. She told me she was well along the road to recovery, and her lively, direct, laughing manner corroborated it, but she still had no place to live.

The next morning, per instructions, I had everyone out at 7:30 although it was snowing lightly and blowing like stink. The kids would go to school and their parents would pursue their lives during the day, looking for work or not, seeking help for those lives or not. Even those who had a fixed destination—school or the day shelter—would likely have to spend some time outside passing through the inclement weather. Try putting a ten-year-old boy and his mother who have spent the night on a gym floor out into the slick, freezing streets, snow coming down, and then see how you feel getting in your car and turning on the heater.

Apart from the role of bad mental or physical health many of us are just a couple of ill-judged financial decisions or a market collapse away from poverty. Rodrigo López's* family was one of these. The family had left the Goose Hollow shelter for housing a little over a month before I met them. They had slept on the church's gym floor for three weeks before a Catholic Charities worker located an apartment for them. Rodrigo and his wife, Silvia*, were both from the Mexican state of Guerrero and had been living and working in Portland without Social Security numbers for over twenty years. They had a fifteen-year-old daughter, Norena*, and a son, Daniel*, who was eleven. The children were both born in Portland and unlike their parents they were U.S. citizens. They grew up in an ample two-bedroom apartment and did well in school.

Rodrigo was short and stocky, fifty-two years old with dark hair combed back and a thick black moustache. He had a business buying "junker" cars from people, which he would then sell for scrap. His wife was a cook at a local Mexican restaurant. They were doing fine, making the rent on the apartment each month with no problem, he told me in Spanish, but they wanted more; they wanted to open their own business together. They saved their money and rented a food truck along with a space to park it.

Portland was one of the first cities in the country where the popularity of food trucks took off, and it is now a solidly rooted culinary tradition. With Silvia cooking and Rodrigo managing they didn't see how they could fail. But they spent all of their savings starting the business, not even keeping enough in reserve to buy an awning for people to stand under while waiting for their orders on rainy days—of which there were many. The family put everything they had into getting the business off the ground, but after a year they ran out of money. They could pay neither the rent on the truck nor the rent on their apartment. They had no income nor any place to live.

"We never imagined that we'd fall into this kind of situation," Rodrigo told me. "It's very easy to become homeless. All of a sudden you have more bills than income, and you can fall into it. It can happen to anyone."[16] The family spent part of August 2014 reduced to living in their car beside a city park. It was a big car, one that Rodrigo had salvaged, a 1979 Chevrolet Impala, but even so it did not have enough room for his family to stretch out while they slept. When I interviewed him in November 2014 he was back at work buying junkers and his wife was cooking for a nearby restaurant. It was cold and snowing on the day I visited the apartment that Catholic Charities had found for the family. His wife had already walked to work but Portland's schools were canceled and the children were home. The wind was blowing hard across the frozen sidewalk in front of the apartment, and it was the kind of day that would make a person particularly grateful for a roof and heat. Rodrigo and the kids sat me down on a broad new sofa in the living room.

The family's stint of homelessness was still fresh in Rodrigo's mind. "What I needed to do was put myself by a freeway exit with a sign asking for help because of my children, but I didn't have the courage to do it. I needed help, but I was ashamed. I parked the car beside a park, and I would put my sign in the window, while the kids played in the park. The sign read: 'Working family of four need help,'" he told me, tears springing into his eyes at the memory, dropping his head for a moment. He paused to recover himself and his daughter, sitting beside him on the sofa, put her hand on his shoulder. A lovely girl with shoulder-length auburn hair, she told me that she wanted to go on to university and become a dentist.

People passing by the car who saw the sign sometimes stopped and gave Rodrigo food and money. Even when the family had enough to pay for food at a fast-food restaurant, they would not go inside. "By the second or third day that you're homeless, in the car with all your clothes, your pots and pans, everything, having to wash yourself in a public rest room, you logically start to feel dirty," Rodrigo said. "You prefer to use the drive-through where no one will see you. You begin to hide your family."

Once the Catholic Charities' caseworker took them on, she got the family a top-priority spot on the waiting list at Goose Hollow and they stayed at the shelter for three weeks before finding the apartment where I spoke with them. "Goose Hollow has a good system; you eat plenty and they have showers. But, it wasn't easy being there with a complete lack of privacy, all the rules they have, to be there in that gymnasium at night watching all the problems in other people's families, between parents and children. It was only logical that we wanted to get out of there as soon as possible. It wears you out.

"We kept right on doing the little work we had. My wife at the restaurant, and I'd chase down any word I had about a junker. I'd go wherever it was they had one for sale, and sometimes we'd get back to the shelter just in time, but we made a little money, and we didn't quit." The caseworker directed them to a rental assistance program, but even with guaranteed funds it was not easy to find a place. "For a little while when we were in the shelter I lost hope of finding anything. Laura [his Catholic Charities caseworker] had to work hard to help us find a place."

About three hundred families receive rental assistance from Multnomah County each year. "We have chosen as a community to not necessarily invest in shelter, but to invest in rapid rehousing," Tiffany Kingery, a program specialist for the county's Homeless Family System of Care, told me in the fall of 2014. "We spend less than sixty thousand dollars a year on motel vouchers compared to approximately two million dollars for our homeless family rent assistance. If you looked at what we pay for shelter, it's certainly less than what we pay to put people in housing; we're really investing in that. So people are often diverted from ever going into shelter and go directly to housing. That's our thinking and our plan."[17]

It sounded good and perhaps it would have worked if enough housing specialists and vacant rental units had been available. They were not, as was indicated by the list of 1,500 families waiting to see one of the handful of housing specialists. Marti Heard, who administers the Title X program with the Portland Public Schools, said the situation for homeless families had reached crisis proportions. "It's just so backlogged that it's completely inefficient right now. It's dire, it really is. There's one side of Portland that everybody's seeing in the media—'Oh, it's wonderful, let's move to Portland'—and then there's an invisible side of Portland that people are not aware of. It's here. It's here, and it's getting worse."[18]

For years policy decisions about Portland's homeless population were split up: the city dealt with homeless individuals, and Multnomah County with homeless families. In an attempt to streamline the system in 2004 all services were accessed through

211, the central intake phone line. In 2014 an agency named JOIN specialized in finding affordable housing for homeless Portland families, while Human Solutions was charged with providing them temporary shelter and rental assistance.

JOIN's director, Marc Jolin, said that the agency did sometimes pay for a family to stay in a motel but it was always a last resort. "We don't really have a motel voucher program. We have the flexibility as providers to put short-term rent assistance into a motel if that is the best option for a family at that moment. The problem is that's four hundred dollars a week, which isn't sustainable in our financial environment.

"Still, if it's a young mom with three kids and she's sleeping in her car where she's super vulnerable, her kids are super vulnerable, and if there's no family member who can put her up, and no other option, we can put her in a motel. But when we do that, given how long it's going to take for her to find housing, we're probably on the hook to that motel for two months of hotel stays. That's a substantial financial investment and that's money we'd rather help her use to pay rent in an actual apartment."[19]

Unfortunately it was not easy to find an "actual apartment" to rent even if the money were available. The rental market in Portland was increasingly tight and private landlords had a sizeable pool of applicants from whom to choose, Jolin told me. He was a tall, sandy-haired man with an open manner, who had been JOIN's executive director for eight years, and he was one of the city's most prominent advocates for homeless families. "The recession was a problem here, but it coincided with an especially tight rental market, especially for those families that were really marginally housed, living month to month. The last five years we've seen almost double-digit rent increases year over year. The demand is huge.

"It's our sense that there are a lot more families living doubled up now than there used to be, many more families economically forced to move back in with family, or to sleep on friends' couches, or to live in a garage. The challenge of finding a unit of rental housing that someone can afford to pay for is tough. Then that family has to get through the rigorous screening process that many landlords have. They're trying to assess risk, and see if this person's going to be a good tenant or not. We've got a lot of families with relatively recent evictions; they've got challenged credit; their employment history isn't strong. So with twenty applicants for every unit that's out there, a homeless family is really hard pressed to be the family chosen for that unit by a landlord."

Both JOIN and Human Solutions were pretty much over-whelmed. For those people waiting to see a housing specialist and whose situations were dire, the Warming Center would keep them from freezing to death at night during the winter. The rest of the year families found shelter as best they could: in motels, cars, camped in the woods, or in a tent along the riverbank.

In late October 2014, just before the winter shelter opened, a friend told me that a friend of hers had reported seeing a homeless man with a toddler camped out down by the river along the Springwater Corridor, a walking and bicycle trail that passes between railroad tracks and the Willamette River's southeastern bank. It is one of a number of places around the city favored by chronically homeless Portlanders for living outdoors.

The day I went over to check it out was coincidentally one day after police and park rangers had come through, warning everyone they found to pack up their tents and their belongings and be gone within twenty-four hours, because if they were still there the next day they would be going to jail. It happened on a regular basis and once a few days had passed people would come back and construct new campsites.

I stopped to ask a trio of two women and a young man if they knew of any parents with children who might be living along the corridor. The three of them were packing up a tent at the top of an embankment with a path leading down to the river; they were folding blankets and sorting through boxes in a desultory manner. One of the women explained that they had to pack up and move before the day ended.

She was a big African American, not obese, simply large with tight salt-and-pepper curls. She wore a denim shirt with the shirttails out, and jeans. Her two companions were a white couple, a skinny man and woman who did not look like they were too long out of their teens and who told me they were from a small town in Colorado. The black woman told me her name was Princess. "The police came through here yesterday, and said that they're going to put us in prison for staying overnight in a public place. The truth is, it's illegal to be homeless," she said, shaking her head at the absurdity of it. She reached into the pocket of her denim shirt and produced a half-smoked joint. "I'm fifty-three, and I'm four months pregnant," she told me as she lit it. "I thought I'd already gone through my change of life and couldn't get pregnant. My mistake. I spent all of last winter here, but it looks like this winter I'll have to find somewhere indoors."

Princess told me that until the police had come through, a man and his toddler son were living further down along the corridor trail, but they had left just after the rousting as had almost everyone else and as she was preparing to do. "The guy said his name was Pirate. I think he said he was going to go over by the

Hawthorne Bridge," she told me, and suggested I look for him there.

I drove over to Hawthorne Street and sure enough it looked like a good possibility: the ground and sidewalks under the bridge were occupied by a couple of tents; a considerable number of people apparently doing nothing more than hanging around; a half dozen supermarket shopping carts scattered about; and a folding table where a church group was distributing sandwiches. I approached a knot of maybe half a dozen younger people gathered around one of the bridge's concrete pillars to ask if any of them knew Pirate. A white girl among them who did not look older than eighteen, brown hair in dreadlocks, shaved at the temples, a teardrop tattooed under one eye, focused on me and before I could say a word she started yelling, "Fuck you. Go away. What do you want? Get out of here, what do you want?"

A guy who looked quite a few years older was standing beside her, leaning on the handlebars of an old bike with chipped red paint, which had seen better days. As had he. He wheeled the bike over to me and got right up in my face. He was pale, lean, hair in a buzz-cut, with crazy brown eyes and a scar from the edge of his forehead to his cheek. "You heard her, didn't you?" he asked, hard, menacing. "Believe me, you don't want to hear her say it again.... Hey," he continued in the same aggressive tone, "how much money you got? What is it you want?"

All I wanted at that moment was to be somewhere else. It felt like methamphetamine violence was in the air around us. I was no longer inclined to see if I could find someone who could tell me where Pirate and his kid might be. The day had turned ugly. In fact I imagined Pirate might not be all that glad to see me even if I did find him.

"Nothing, I don't want anything," I told him, turning my back and walking away. He didn't follow.

. . .

In the years between the 1909 White House Conference and the Great Depression of 1929 much of the nation prospered at record levels, accumulating great wealth in the stock market. However a substantial underclass of people existed who could not keep even a tenement roof over their heads or those of their families. As always, racial minorities and recently arrived immigrants had the hardest time finding the wherewithal to get by. While many people made fortunes during the 1920s, millions more did not have enough to feed their families. It was a situation not unlike the years from the late 1990s through 2006, prosperous years of growing wealth for some Americans while at the same time the number of poor and homeless families continued to grow.

When the stock market imploded in 1929 the number of desperate families skyrocketed. Suddenly so many people were in need of assistance that municipalities and states were overwhelmed, unable to provide for all those who needed help. President Herbert Hoover staunchly believed that private charities and local governments had to take responsibility for the unemployed and homeless. As unemployment soared he continued to insist that charities and local funds could take care of those who were out of work and struggling. "I am confident," said Hoover in 1931, "that our people have the resources, the initiative, the courage, the stamina and kindliness of spirit to meet this situation in the way they have met their problems over generations."[20]

In 1931 food riots erupted in places like Oklahoma City and Minneapolis; shops and grocery stores were looted by people desperate to feed themselves and their children. In 1933 as the

Great Depression swept millions into poverty, some 20 percent of the nation's children who did attend school were not receiving the daily nutrition, housing, or medical care they needed according to the federal Children's Bureau.[21] In many cities people had lost their homes and were living in outdoor encampments that came to be known as "Hoovervilles." The inhabitants were out of work and spent their days looking for enough to feed their families. Many youngsters were pulled out of school and sent out to earn pennies.

By 1932 only one in every four unemployed families received any form of relief. As Franklin Roosevelt took office some fourteen million American workers were unemployed, amounting to 25 percent of white adult males and 50 percent of African American adult males.[22] With their husbands out of work wives took whatever income they could find. African American women found work as domestic servants and cooks or took in washing. In addition many men simply abandoned their homes, leaving behind "grass widows" either out of a desire to rid themselves or their families of a burden. A survey in 1940 found 1.5 million married women who had been abandoned by their husbands.[23]

In 1934, the second year of Roosevelt's New Deal, forty-six out of forty-eight states had some type of mother's pension. While this assistance helped, it was often not enough, nor did it extend to all who were in equal need. In 1934 the average mother's pension amounted to eleven dollars per month and even that was frequently denied to mothers who had divorced or were African American.[24] Across the nation the amounts varied by state. In 1933, at the height of the Depression, Louisiana's average monthly expenditure per family was $8.81, and it was $51.83 in Massachusetts.[25] As small as some of the assistance sums may have been, deep in the Depression every little bit helped.

By 1933 more than half the nation's children were growing up in families that did not have enough money to pay for food, shelter, clothing, and medical care.[26] Many of these children opted for life on their own or were forced to do so. Times were tremendously tough and children keenly felt the privations of their families. Some were pushed out and many more left voluntarily, glad to trade in a family's life of poverty and hunger for the unknown and the independence of life on the road.

These days once again the number of unaccompanied youth under eighteen is growing annually. Many of these kids have run away from dysfunctional families where as many as 60 percent report physical abuse and 40 percent say they were abused sexually.[27] Others have been thrown out of their families because of substance abuse issues or because their sexual orientations are other than strictly straight.

The problem has been growing for decades. An estimated one million kids were homeless and on their own for at least one night over the course of 1995. In 2014 the National Association for the Education of Homeless Children and Youth estimated that as many as 1.7 million young people under eighteen were living on their own at some time during the year.[28] While a 2012 study found that most spent less than a week on their own, some 380,000 were without family for over a week, and over the course of a year about 130,000 kids lived on their own for longer than a month.[29] These homeless, unaccompanied youth are difficult to count accurately because like homeless families they have a vested interest in remaining invisible to the authorities and are frequently skilled at doing so.

Even more difficult to accurately count and more determined to evade detection are the numbers of unaccompanied and undocumented youth who arrive from Central America and

Mexico. Some one hundred thousand are expected to cross the border in 2015, while a decade before that only about a thousand kids a year were doing so, according to journalist Maria Hinojosa, who has studied the issue in depth.[30] Precise counts of homeless minors, whether citizens or undocumented immigrants, do not exist.

It was equally impossible during the Great Depression to know how many youngsters under the age of eighteen were living on their own, but estimates were that 250,000 minors were wandering the country at loose ends, riding their thumbs or the rails, struggling to maintain body and soul on a daily basis.[31] Children jumping on freight trains was a common sight in any railroad yard. Many of these kids moved from place to place, staying alive by their wits or the kindness of strangers. Many of them had voluntarily left home so as to remove an extra mouth to feed at the family board, convinced that somewhere else, anywhere else, they would find employment. Most of this wave of homeless youngsters comprised boys, but girls too hit the road.

Thomas Minehan, a graduate student in the sociology department at the University of Minnesota, traveled with these youngsters over the course of holidays and summer vacations, catching freight trains with them and sleeping huddled up in out-of-the-way corners. He collected over five hundred case histories in 1932 and 1933 and wrote them down. "One of the first facts I learned was that a great number of homeless men were youths and even boys.... And as I left the mission district to live in hobo railroad yard camps or jungles and river shanty-towns, I found more and more youths and not a few girls," he wrote in 1934.[32]

Life on the road was not easy and Minehan noted that for the first six months kids were often enthusiastic and excited about their newfound independence, but after that they began to yearn for another, more stable kind of life. After a half year they had begun to have a greater appreciation and fear of the perils that attended the lives they were living. By that time they had gone hungry and been apprehended and beaten by railroad yard police. They had crossed paths with boys and girls who told how they had been robbed and raped, and others who had seen kids die of fever or crushed beneath the wheels of a freight train. Between 1929 and 1939 almost twenty-five thousand "trespassers" of all ages died in railroad yard accidents across the nation, with almost twenty-eight thousand injured according to Interstate Commerce Commission figures.[33]

In 1935 the Social Security Act was passed, guaranteeing an income for the old, the disabled, and single mothers in deep poverty. The act was the cornerstone of Roosevelt's New Deal and went a long way toward lifting millions out of desperate circumstances. Title IV of the act established Aid to Dependent Children, later renamed Aid to Families with Dependent Children (AFDC).

Initially AFDC was intended to pay one-third of a state's costs for mothers' pensions. Unfortunately it also allowed states to continue determining eligibility criteria, meaning that in many places African American mothers continued to receive little or none of the available funds. Nor was just being white always enough to qualify a mother for assistance. In numerous states "cohabitation" with a man was grounds for a mother's ineligibility, and in some places cohabitation was defined as any sexual relationship outside of marriage. Over three decades in Alabama this regulation alone made sixteen thousand children ineligible for AFDC, until the Supreme Court prohibited the cohabitation standard, ruling that the provision punished a woman for engaging in sexual relations and was unrelated to Congress's intent to provide aid to needy children.[34] Despite the drawbacks of AFDC its creation by the federal government would ease the lives of millions of families over the decades ahead.

Even after Roosevelt was elected and radically changed the federal government's policies, the Depression did not end for everyone until 1940 when the burgeoning prewar economy began to fill the nation's coffers and employ its youth. World War Two brought its own set of tragedies but also initiated an era of prosperity that would continue more or less unabated for decades, outlasting various mini-recessions, the Cold War, a gas shortage, and two long and costly wars right up until 1980.

In 1964 Lyndon Johnson's War on Poverty widened the scope of Roosevelt-era programs and committed federal funding to a range of new measures. Johnson's policies expanded federal responsibility for those who could not help themselves: both the working poor and those who could not or would not work. The Medicare and Medicaid health-care programs were created as well as food stamps. In April 1965, after less than a year of the food stamp program's existence, five hundred thousand people were signed up according to government statistics. By 2008 the number had risen to twenty nine million, and in 2013 a staggering forty-seven million people—almost one-sixth of the country—participated in the food stamp program.[35]

Another component of the War on Poverty was the Head Start program, which was designed to meet the emotional, social, health, nutritional, and psychological needs of children between the ages of three and five who live in poverty. By 2013 nearly a million children were in Head Start programs, for which the budget was about $6.5 billion.[36] When spending on Head Start was reauthorized in 2007, Congress specified that special efforts to identify and serve homeless children had to be made by existing programs and that all new programs applying for Head Start funding had to provide a plan to meet the needs of homeless children and children in foster care, including transportation needs.[37]

.   .   .

The 1909 White House Conference set a precedent and for the next six decades the White House convened a conference every ten years to address issues of caring for poor children. The 1909 conference had some 215 attendees and the 1971 edition, presided over by Richard Nixon, had more than a thousand invitees. It was the last one. Ronald Reagan did not see fit to carry on the tradition.

With Reagan's election in 1980 the government began to reverse course and reduce federal responsibility for poor children. Lyndon Johnson's vision of the government in a war against poverty began to be eroded during the Reagan years, which were more focused on promoting prosperity among the privileged, assuring the public that it would trickle down. Federal poverty programs were cut back and eliminated when possible. Deregulation and privatization began the process of putting public wealth in private hands, a process that inevitably increased the numbers of extremely poor, and extremely rich, people. The federal government shrugged its shoulders at the growth in numbers of single-mother homeless families. Welfare became a dirty word. Our War on Poverty was over. We had lost. Another Gilded Age began.

The dismantling of the federal government's involvement with dependent children was a bipartisan effort. Bill Clinton's 1996 welfare/workfare reforms eliminated the Aid to Families with Dependent Children (AFDC) program, which had been in place since 1935, replacing it with Temporary Assistance for Needy Families (TANF). TANF has proven much less helpful to the poorest of the nation's poor, those families living on a cash budget of less than two dollars a day. The authors of *$2.00 a Day: Living on Almost Nothing in America* wrote: "As of early 1996, the old welfare program was lifting more than a million households with children out of $2-a-day poverty every month.... By mid-2011, TANF was lifting only about 300,000 households with children above the $2-a-day mark."[38]

Extremely poor families were not the only group of people to suffer long-term hardship as the federal government reduced its responsibility for the less fortunate. The mentally ill were largely abandoned to their luck. The State of California began emptying its larger mental institutions in the early 1960s, paying to warehouse mentally ill people in small, often inadequate group homes, even before Reagan became governor in 1967. He encouraged the trend. New York State followed suit: between 1965 and 1977 more than a hundred thousand patients were released from state psychiatric hospitals and perhaps forty-seven thousand of them ended up in New York City.[39]

Federal funding for mental institutions was slashed using the argument that putting these people back into society with adequate resources such as counseling, housing, and job opportunities was better than warehousing them. It might have been but the promise of help for patients once they were out on the streets was not kept. By the end of Reagan's first term in the White House many mentally ill people who had nowhere to live were showing up on city streets. The Reagan administration showed little interest in tackling the problem. The great majority of former patients were left to fend for themselves, a small federal Supplemental Security Income (SSI) monthly check the most they could hope for, guaranteed to keep them poor and struggling. Many of them have lived on our streets ever since.

Provisions for treatment of the mentally ill have always been closely tied to those for homeless families, and public policy toward one group has often reflected public policy toward the other. Many times over the course of our nation's history, care was provided in the same place and the mentally ill slept and ate with the homeless poor. Now once again, as two hundred years ago in the earliest nineteenth-century almshouses, children in need of emergency shelter are housed with the mentally ill.

It should come as no surprise that some of the parents heading the families filling emergency shelters are struggling with mental and emotional issues. Depression among female heads of homeless families is disproportionately higher than among housed mothers according to a study published in 2014, coauthored by Ellen Bassuk: "Homeless mothers experience disproportionately high rates of major depressive disorder compared with the general population. Stressed by their circumstances, these women struggle to protect their families. Children living with a depressed parent have poorer medical, mental health, and educational outcomes. Despite the adverse impact on children, depression among mothers experiencing homelessness remains unacknowledged, unrecognized, and untreated."[40]

It is not hard to imagine that even those homeless mothers who do not have debilitating mental issues are at greater risk of developing them than poor women who are housed. Resources dedicated to treatment and prevention of depression among heads of homeless families are slim and Bassuk's study called for a recognition of the problem as a high public health priority, including training for the staffs of social service agencies in dealing with major depression. She cited studies concluding that when depression is recognized and treated in mothers their children will develop fewer emotional and behavioral problems.

Since 1980, year after year, about half of all poor families are maintained by single mothers. These women are often ill equipped to deal with the stress and expenses of caring for children while holding down a minimum-wage job. Homelessness makes it all that much harder. Single mothers in homeless families have been robbed, raped, and beaten more often than poor women who live in poverty but are housed. Violence as well as incidents of emotional, physical, and sexual abuse in both children and adults are more common in the lives of homeless women than in those of their housed economic counterparts.[41]

Obviously all of these factors can generate mental and emotional problems, yet many of the staff at emergency shelters across the nation have little or no training in how to recognize and treat depressed or mentally unstable mothers, women whose children are depending on them for their daily survival. Even if some kind of training or therapy is available through the shelter where they are staying, they may not have time in their lives to take advantage of it. And that's the case for women staying in shelters. A mother living in a car or motel room with her family is likely to have even less opportunity to deal with her own mental health issues or those of her children.

A growing body of evidence makes it clear that the stress engendered by extreme poverty and homelessness has measurably toxic effects on children, not only on their minds but also on their bodies. For instance in a forty-two-year study initiated in 1972 and reported in a 2014 *Science* article, five thousand poor North Carolina children up to the age of five were provided full day care, three meals a day, a lot of conversation, and mental stimulation. Five thousand others were provided only with adequate nutrition.

The study was designed to see what effect the difference in treatment would have on intelligence. In fact those in the nurtured group were four times more likely to attend college. However researchers were surprised also to find a significant difference in physical health after four decades. Those who had received full day care had far less cases of obesity, high blood pressure, and high cholesterol levels after forty-two years. The group also had far better levels of "good" cholesterol. "This tells us that adversity does matter, and that it does affect adult health," James Heckman, a University of Chicago economics professor and lead data analyst for the study, told the *New York Times*. "But it also shows us that we can do something about it, that poverty is not just a hopeless condition."[42]

CHAPTER FIVE

Trenton, New Jersey

Rapid Rehousing

"This is not the first time in our history that widening
socio-economic gaps have threatened our economy,
our democracy, and our values. The specific responses
we have pursued to successfully overcome these
challenges and restore opportunity have varied in
detail, but underlying them all was a commitment to
invest in other people's children. And underlying that
commitment was a deeper sense that those kids, too,
were our kids.

Our Kids, Robert Putnam (2015)[1]

As Martin Luther King, Jr., told us so clearly in 1968, the question
is not whether we *can* end family homelessness. We know how to
do it. The question is whether we have the will. This is a challeng-
ing time. Funds to help homeless families are meager at the federal, state, and local levels and most of the assistance programs are
carried out in the well-worn grooves of outdoor or indoor relief
using one of their limited contemporary variations, all of them
inadequate: emergency shelters, motels, TANF (Temporary
Assistance for Needy Families), or foster care.

When funds *are* dedicated to addressing homelessness they are often spent in the service of more visible, chronically homeless individuals instead of families. All the while, more and more wage earners find that a forty-hour work week in the service sector doesn't come close to paying their family's rent, food, and expenses. In 2014 a person who spent the federally recommended 30 percent of earnings on rent would have had to make $18.92 an hour to pay fair market rental on a two-bedroom apartment in any city in the United States according to the National Low-Income Housing Coalition—an increase of 52 percent since 2000.[2]

That is a lot more than minimum wage and in many places it's more than what two people earning minimum wage would bring home. It is not surprising that many families go through a patch of homelessness. In some ways they have less recourse than a nineteenth-century family did in similar straits. For the latter, orphanages often served as a safety valve and it was not only children without parents who lived in them. Children were often placed in such an institution if the family was going through a particularly difficult financial crisis. When a single parent or a two-parent family was suffering financial reverses and could not keep a child fed and clothed, they could leave the child at an orphanage until things got better, perhaps contributing what they could toward upkeep.

While widowed or abandoned women were the groups most likely to temporarily deposit their children at an orphanage for a period of time, men too regularly turned up with their offspring. Death in childbirth was common and illness also carried off its share of young mothers. Those widowers who did not remarry quickly often found themselves emotionally and financially overwhelmed. Even if a man had a job he might be hard pressed to find care for his children while he worked, and it was no easy task to feed a family at the end of a long, hard workday. In such straits single fathers often turned to an orphanage. In a sense these orphanages were like boarding schools for the poor, where children were housed and fed until they were reclaimed.

This was a commonly employed strategy for getting a family through hard times, a sort of temporary custody that was generally accepted as part and parcel of an orphanage's mission. It is worth noting that currently, although times are no less hard for many people, no such temporary recourse exists. If a parent is having trouble caring for a child and asks for help, the child is likely to be taken into the foster care system and the mother or father may have a difficult time regaining custody. By contrast, in the last two decades of the nineteenth century a child at the Albany Orphan Asylum in upstate New York could be reclaimed and brought home with as little as two weeks' written notice to the institution.[3]

Innovative public policy toward family homelessness is a rare beast. In most places public officials turn to emergency shelters—indoor relief—or foster care to deal with extremely poor families and their children. Many of the people providing social services to homeless families do not have time to read about innovative policies being carried out elsewhere, much less think about implementing those policies in their own communities. What they are doing with their time in many places is fighting a rearguard action to keep their already inadequate funding and programs from being slashed yet again, defending themselves against attacks by those who would have them work with even less resources.

Today many politicians still subscribe to the ideas of Herbert Hoover and Franklin Pierce. Take Missouri for instance where in May 2015 the heavily Republican state legislature passed a bill reducing by 20 percent the amount of time a poor family could draw TANF, and instituting work requirements for food stamp recipients. The TANF benefits were already low: $292 a month for a single parent with two children. The new legislation, which was passed by overriding a Democrat governor's veto, would cut benefits to about three thousand of the state's families, including more than six thousand children.[4]

Missouri's Republican state senator David Sater was the bill's author. "Currently, the way things are, a person can apply for TANF benefits for their family, and not participate in any work activity at all," he told a reporter for *Heartlander Magazine*. "I want to see people going back to work, and more people being less dependent on government for their existence, and I think this bill will go a long way in that direction."[5]

Fortunately that's not the only direction in which state and local governments are going. Some places across the nation, like Fairfax, Virginia, have opted for trying new models to reduce family homelessness. They have decided to apply a collective will to see that children in their communities do not have to sleep in cars, shelters, motels, or packed in with relatives. These places are attempting to eliminate family homelessness to the extent that public funds can do so, and they are developing cost-effective means by which most homeless families can acquire housing and stay in it.

The policy of choice in such locations is rapid rehousing.

In Mercer County, New Jersey, officials were enthusiastically putting it into practice. Like Fairfax County, Mercer was one of the richest counties per capita in the entire nation, home to a number of multinational corporate headquarters and Princeton University, which reported an $18.7 billion endowment in 2013.

Cheek by jowl with this massive wealth were numerous homeless families, "frail forms fainting at the door" as Stephen Foster penned it. The city of Trenton with a population of eighty-five thousand was the Mercer County seat and also New Jersey's capital city. It was only nine miles down the road from Princeton's manicured, stately campus, but some parts of Trenton looked like a war zone.

Apart from the office buildings that surrounded the New Jersey capitol building like pilot fish swimming alongside a shark, the city consisted mostly of bad neighborhoods, boarded-up store fronts, way too many young people hanging out on the sidewalks, and block after block with a pervasive air of collapse and abandonment. Trenton's murder rate was more than four times higher than New Jersey's average and its crime rate was one of the highest in the nation for a city its size.[6] The chances of being assaulted within its precincts were three times the national average. In 2014 unemployment in New Jersey was 9 percent but in Trenton it was 14 percent. The annual median income for people living in Trenton was barely half that of those in the rest of Mercer County.

Trenton's population of homeless families was not new. As far back as 1987 Tricia Fagan, executive director of a New Jersey advocacy group, Right to Housing, told an interviewer: "All over the state, there are families in hotels and motels, and they're unable to find housing. There's a real need to look at housing policy in this state.... Something's got to be done because these people are not going away."[7]

And of course they didn't go away. Fifteen years later in 2002 Trenton had the second-highest rate of family homelessness in the nation. Mercer County's Board of Social Services was spending upward of $12 million a year funding shelters, and when those were full the board paid $75 a night to house overflow families in motels along Route One. On any given night in 2002 some nine hundred people were homeless and almost 50 percent of them were children. A group of 150 community organizations was formed to respond to the situation, including people from city and county government, nonprofits, universities, churches, and businesses. They participated in drafting a ten-year plan to end homelessness in Mercer County, which led to the formation in 2004 of the Mercer Alliance to End Homelessness.[8]

As the 2007 recession ran its course, its effects were felt even in prosperous Mercer County. Still the 2009 point-in-time count showed only a moderate increase in homelessness: a total of 1,067 homeless individuals, 355 of whom were children while 240 more were heads of families. In that year, halfway to the end of the ten-year plan, the alliance issued a revised version. It no longer envisioned ending homelessness but rather enumerated some more nuanced and attainable goals: "Mercer County will demonstrate that we can prevent homelessness in many instances, shorten homelessness when it cannot be avoided and provide permanent housing with supportive services to both individuals and families as quickly as possible."

By 2011 the homeless population was reduced to 843 individuals, of whom 269 were children. In 2014 the Mercer Alliance reported a 58 percent decline in homelessness since 2007. The main tool used was rapid rehousing and the county became a kind of proving ground to see if a housing-first strategy was effective in reducing the number of homeless families. In 2013 the National Alliance to End Homelessness evaluated Mercer County's program: "Rapid Rehousing is helping families quickly and successfully exit homelessness and the vast majority of families stays housed. To date, less than 5 percent of rapidly re-housed families have returned to shelter."[9]

For a long time the county was just treading water in dealing with its homeless population according to Marygrace Billek, Mercer County's director of human services. "Historically, we spent a great deal of time managing homelessness here. We decided in 2007 that was a bad idea; we didn't want to do that anymore. At that time, the National Alliance to End Homelessness was coming out with some of its 'best practices.' We used ARRA [American Recovery and Reinvestment Act] stimulus money in 2009, and we got some federal grant money, and tried rapid rehousing.

"We focused on families because they were easier to deal with," she told me in May 2014. "They are not mentally ill, and they may have substance use issues, rather than substance abuse issues. There's very little difference between the families that are poor in Trenton, and families that are homeless, except for a job lost, or a car broke down. Those are the reasons a family is homeless."[10]

The university dedicated little attention or money to saving Trenton, generally ignoring the urban blight at its doorstep. When I asked Billek if she got a lot of help from Princeton, a look of disgust passed quickly across her face. "All I need to tell you is that you can't send your kids to school in Trenton. It's terrible." She was coming from a morning meeting with other Trenton community leaders discussing the recent death of a sixteen-year-old, an innocent bystander shot in the head during a drive-by shooting. It was not the first such meeting she'd been to, by any means, and she said she was tired of it. "There's got to be something better we can do. We need to be thinking about that."

One reason that rapid rehousing was easier in Mercer County than in many other places was Trenton's depressed housing market. In Princeton real estate prices were on a par with those of

New York City but the housing market in Trenton, nine miles away, more closely resembled Detroit than Manhattan. Between June 2010 and April 2013, 359 families went through Mercer County's rapid rehousing program. Only 6 percent of them had fallen back into homelessness and 82 percent had exited rapid rehousing into stable housing according to Billek. The average length of a shelter stay was reduced from eighty-seven to fifty-six days.

"What has happened is sort of amazing," she told me. "The homeless family population is down more than seventy-one percent. It's true that rapid rehousing does not work for everyone. About ten percent of our families need lots of services to avoid being chronically homeless. Primary housing is not appropriate for them. But with the other ninety percent, get them in a house, put them in a house, and most of them will stay in that house."

For the 10 percent of families not equipped to move into a place of their own, Mercer County had Connie Mercer. Her married name was a coincidence—neither she nor her husband were Mercer County natives but they had lived there a long time. As the founder and executive director of a nonprofit named HomeFront she had worked with the county's homeless families since 1992. Up until then she had owned a head-hunting agency but her life changed when a pediatrician friend took her on a tour of a Trenton she had never seen.

"He told me, 'You need to see what's going on in your community,'" she recalled. "What I saw horrified me. About two hundred families who were housed in grim motels along the Route One corridor. My friend said, 'There are hungry, homeless kids in your town. Fix it.' And that's when it all started. I thought all I would need to do to fix it would be to tell everybody about it, in this incredibly wealthy community with Princeton at its heart."[11]

Twenty-two years later she was still at it, and in 2014 Home-Front had evolved from its 1992 version of a small band of volunteers serving meals to homeless families into an agency that on any given day provided shelter to about 450 people, two-thirds of them children. HomeFront's main shelter, named the Family Preservation Center, offered thirty-eight different programs for its population, ranging from preschool and summer camps for homeless kids to budgeting skills, job readiness, art therapy, and literacy classes for their parents. Many of the heads of families at the shelter read at a fifth-grade level, not sufficiently high to qualify for anything but minimum-wage work. The computer room had forty computers and the library's shelves had a lot of books for both adults and children. The shelter could house a maximum of forty families at a time and was almost always full. Mercer referred to it as the "Ritz-Carlton of shelters."

For all of that, Cheryl Jefferson*, an eighteen-year-old African American mother of an almost two-year-old daughter, was looking forward to leaving the shelter and moving into her own apartment. She had been at the Family Preservation Center for only three weeks before being rapidly rehoused. "My mom and I got into a very bad argument and she just told me to get out, and not come back,"[12] she told me.

"When she threw me out, I was homeless, going from house to house, staying a night with friends. When I got here I was broken, broken by the things that had happened to me. The programs and classes here are helping me get out all that hurt inside, all that negative energy that I had, so I can bring in some good energy." Cheryl was an attractive, slender young woman with long black hair and lively, engaged, measuring eyes. She had never held a job nor lived by herself. She had been in school all her life and when we spoke at the shelter she had just finished her first year at Mercer Community College studying criminal justice. An apartment had already been found for her and she would shortly be moving out of the shelter to live on her own with her daughter.

"It's true it will be my first time living on my own, but I don't think it will be much of a challenge. At my mother's house, I was kind of the mother of that house. I kept up with the bills and did the house cleaning. One thing I'm going to do is keep coming back here for classes. They're very helpful." One thing she said she will not do in the near future is have any more babies. "The one I've got feels like two. Seriously. I have child care because I'm in college, but she's still a handful. I don't have time to be in another relationship. Right now, it's all about me."

Sheila Addison was the manager of HomeFront's Family Preservation Center, where she had worked for ten years. In her opinion the best thing for many young women like Cheryl would be more time getting ready to leave the shelter, preparing for life on her own. However she also acknowledged that more and more of the families at the shelter were people who had spent years living on their own, raising their families in safe, secure environments, who would never have imagined themselves without a home. "When the economy changed, the look of the homeless changed. It became middle class: teachers who had gotten laid off, people like that. More people needing food bags and clothes. It was no longer the person in the corner of the bus terminal, but your middle-class person. Even with rapid rehousing, our beds here stay full."

Connie Mercer echoed her manager's sentiments. She was not as enthusiastic about rapid rehousing as many others in Mercer County. "We love rapid rehousing for the right family. However, it's not a silver bullet. There are families that need much more.

Most eighteen-year-old kids that already have three babies need more than just thirty days in a shelter, and then to be put into housing. They know it, and when their case managers come and yank them out of our place in the name of rapid rehousing, them screaming, 'I don't want to go!' I'm not sure it's the best public policy."

One Mercer County Alliance member I spoke with said of Connie Mercer, "She's a housing-readiness provider, not a housing-first person. Some of our provider agencies still operate on the premise that they know best, a little maternalistic or paternalistic." At any rate there were enough homeless families to go around. In 2014 HomeFront's shelters were almost always full and the alliance had a steady stream of mothers and children who needed housing. However the number of families receiving emergency shelter in those Route One motels had been reduced to virtually zero. "The only reason that a family should be in a motel has to do with if there's a young man—fourteen, fifteen, sixteen years of age—living in the family. Connie Mercer's shelter doesn't allow young men living in it, so we direct them to a motel until some other accommodation is available," said Marygrace Billek.

Another advantage to the rapid rehousing policy, she told me, was cost. "We've shown that it's cheaper to put somebody in rapid rehousing than to put them in an emergency shelter. Rapid rehousing costs fifty dollars a day, which includes twenty-five for rent and twenty-five for case management, as opposed to one hundred twenty-five dollars, which is the minimum for emergency shelter, and eighty-four dollars a day to keep a family in transitional housing."

Emergency shelter systems across the country often include some form of transitional housing, either individual subsidized or congregate units designed to house families for a limited time—often a year or two at the outside—while they hone their living skills and prepare for a move into permanent housing. In the recent past transitional housing was an integral part of many systems dealing with homeless families, and it is still frequently advocated by housing-readiness proponents. Mercer County has reduced its transitional housing and for those families that still pass through it the average length of time a family stays in transitional housing has been cut substantially, from 253 to 143 days.

So which model works better for families dealing with homelessness, rapid rehousing or housing readiness? Outdoor relief or indoor relief? It is one of the questions that has vexed public policy makers since the first white settlers came to Virginia and Massachusetts. How and whether to provide shelter for those who cannot provide it for themselves have been recurring questions throughout our history. In our day early returns from those communities that have put rapid rehousing into effect indicate that most family homelessness in the twenty-first century is in fact simply an economic problem, a result of being too poor to afford a place to rent. That is certainly true for the hundreds of thousands of families who have experienced homelessness even while a parent was holding down a full-time job at minimum wage.

More than a century ago the 1909 White House Conference report condemned the practice of keeping desperately poor children and their families in congregate housing, calling it "an unqualified evil." For much of the twentieth century, almshouses virtually disappeared from our landscapes. The few shelters that existed were used primarily by homeless single men. However since the 1980s and the Reagan era when homeless families began to appear in numbers, public policy for dealing with them at the local level has often provided little more than basic shelter. Just keeping the growing numbers of women and children under a roof became an expensive and unwelcome responsibility for cities and towns, places where it had never before been necessary. In many locales punitive, tight-fisted public officials offered homeless families only the shelter alternative. As a result youngsters were often condemned to living part of their childhood in some nasty places, extremely unhealthy environments in which to grow up.

In many of our communities more and more families are priced out of housing, more and more working poor people fall into poverty, struggling to get by with the little they have, which buys them less and less. All the while the rest of us prosper. If we are going to adapt ourselves to the increasing gulf between rich and poor, mustn't we at least collectively decide not to tolerate children living in cars or being raised in motel rooms or emergency shelters?

Turning It Around

Only slightly over a century ago desperately poor young children were expected to go to work wherever and whenever they could. Child labor was an accepted part of the nation's economic structure. As late as 1904 Robert Hunter wrote that eighty thousand children were employed in textile mills in the South, most of them young girls. Things were no better in the North: in Pennsylvania 120,000 children were working in the mining regions, including 17,000 "little girls" working in the huge silk mills and lace factories while the boys went down in the coal mines.[1] Huge numbers of children reported daily to full-time jobs that were monotonous, grueling, and sometimes dangerous.

As we have seen, over the course of the twentieth century the notion that children were nothing more than miniature adults gave way to the idea that childhood is a special time of life, which deserves a different sort of attention and nurturing from that of adulthood. To our twenty-first-century eyes it appears coarse and brutal that parents could have sent their seven-, eight-, and nine-year-olds to work no matter how desperate the family might have been. Perhaps it will seem equally coarse and brutal to North Americans in the twenty-second century that we allowed millions of children to spend part of their lives growing up homeless.

They are likely to wonder why we did not do all we could to eradicate family homelessness. Much of the responsibility for that failure falls today, as it has over the entire history of our nation, on those who believe that public assistance saps the will of the poor and encourages their tendencies toward laziness. Those policy makers opposed to outdoor relief and rent subsidies assert that if the rent can be paid without working, many people will not bother to look for a job. They hold that the poor and homeless are that way through their own faults and that subsidies simply encourage their vices.

In fact raising a family without a stable roof overhead is hard work, as anyone who has had to do it will testify. All of life's quotidian tasks are more time consuming and stressful; the logistics of getting by day to day with too little money leave little room for relaxation and family fun. Nevertheless opponents of public assistance use virtually the same language in their arguments today as was used by those opposed to outdoor relief in the early 1800s. "The demoralization of the poor through the erosion of independence and self-respect; the spread of idleness and the loss of the will to work; the promotion of immorality in all of its ugly forms; and the increases in public costs through the growth of poorhouses and jails; these, so its opponents believed, were the consequences of outdoor relief," wrote Michael Katz.[2]

Presumably even those people who hold that homeless families are responsible for their own predicaments would not advocate leaving them entirely on their own to raise their children in the streets, if only for the sake of the children. But they might well assert that if homeless families must be cared for from the public till it should be done in congregate housing, providing little more than basic food and shelter as cheaply as possible. In the face of a growing population of homeless parents and children the response of a certain segment of our policy makers is the same today as it has been for more than three hundred years: put them in an almshouse.

It is undeniable that the laziest among us have always been willing to take it easy and live by the sweat and taxes of others. Among the desperately poor are people who could be working just like we are but instead choose to indulge their vices while our taxes support them. Lazy people who exploit the system will always exist. How and whether we should separate the "deserving" and "undeserving" poor is not an easy question to resolve. That is why we as a body politic have gone back and forth about it for centuries, trying first one thing then another.

Bill Clinton's 1996 welfare reform mandated that the unemployed able-bodied people who receive public assistance must be looking or training for a job. However nothing guarantees that those who do find minimum-wage work, who are on their feet all day with no health benefits or job security, will make enough of a salary to keep their families under a roof. It is one thing to advocate that the "undeserving" poor should receive no assistance from public monies and quite another to be unwilling to fund more than congregate housing for the family of a minimum-wage worker. Should a parent who spends eight hours a day working hard with no job security or benefits have to spend nights with her children in a shelter?

In January 1963 the *New Yorker* published a review by Dwight MacDonald of Michael Harrington's groundbreaking book about poor people, *The Other America,* published the year before Lyndon

Johnson declared the War on Poverty: "Mr. Harrington estimates that between forty and fifty million Americans, or about a fourth of the population, are now living in poverty. Not just below the level of comfortable living, but real poverty, in the old-fashioned sense of the word—that they are hard put to it to get the mere necessities, beginning with enough to eat. This is difficult to believe in the United States of 1963, but one has to make the effort, and it is now being made. The extent of our poverty has suddenly become visible."[3]

Not visible enough, as it turned out. It is long past time for us to confront the desperate realities of homeless families, this invisible nation that exists around us. Herbert Hoover was right in one sense: the solution to caring for those who cannot care for themselves is ultimately a local one. The federal government may provide the lion's share of funding, but for that money to really contribute to ending family homelessness the residents of each community will have to agree that they will do what it takes to see that children do not go homeless among them. This needs to be a priority at the municipal level. Federal funds must then be spent judiciously and in accordance with best practices.

The federal government can lead the way, and some logical and fundable solutions which would not require any additional taxes have already been proposed to do so. In July 2008, Congress passed the Housing and Economic Recovery Act. Among its provisions was the establishment of a National Housing Trust Fund (NHTF) to create affordable housing, which was to receive its funding from a tiny fraction of the mortgage loans financed by the federal lenders, Fannie Mae and Freddie Mac. The legislation was passed amid the Great Recession and the meltdown of the housing market, so the funding provision was suspended. The two lending entities shortly returned to profitability but funding remained suspended.

New business activity for Fannie Mae and Freddie Mac in 2012 was approximately $1.4 trillion according to the Securities and Exchange Commission. Under the legislation approximately $382 million of that amount would have gone to the NHTF that year.[4] Since 2010 the president has annually included one billion dollars for the fund in his budgets. This would pay for sixteen thousand units of affordable housing according to estimates by the Department of Housing and Urban Development, but Congress has blocked it.[5] In fact in recent years legislation has been introduced, though not yet passed, to eliminate the fund entirely, to abolish it before it ever generates a dollar for affordable housing. Conservative think tanks like the Heritage Foundation have urged Congress to "keep the housing spigot turned off."[6]

However in December 2014 the suspension was finally lifted and money began flowing into the trust fund, with the first distribution of block grants to the states scheduled for 2016. The states would then award grants locally, with at least 80 percent of the money dedicated to rental housing for extremely poor people. It could be used to build new housing, renovate old housing, or subsidize rentals.

Congressional conservatives reacted quickly and by June 2015 they inserted a Republican-sponsored provision in a spending bill, passed by the House, that would have diverted NHTF funds to another federal housing program not focused on the poorest of the poor and prohibited the fund from receiving monies from any other programs. A number of other proposals have been put forth to generate monies for the NHTF at little or no cost to the taxpayer. All of these would have been prohibited under the provision, which would have effectively killed the fund.[7] Over the following months a bipartisan congressional effort succeeded in defeating this provision and protecting the NHTF's level of funding through 2016.

If we want to end family homelessness we need to put families into housing, provide social services to the 10 to 15 percent who will need them, and provide the other 85 percent of families with rental assistance. Studies indicate that most of them will stay housed even after subsidies run out.[8] In the short run the rent subsidies may cost communities more than if they do little or nothing, although innovative solutions like the National Housing Trust Fund can ameliorate those costs. Social services and housing cost money; they demand public resources and public commitment. But in the long run they also make economic sense. Crime is reduced, emergency room visits decrease, and prison costs are lower.

While policy choices often reflect political affiliations this is not really a political issue. Millions of children in our country are unnecessarily suffering hardships, difficulties, and levels of toxic stress that should not be borne by kids. They are going through this on a daily basis not far from where you and I live relatively comfortable lives. Children in the United States should not have to grow up this way. We must do everything possible to make the invisible nation visible so that we can deal with it and put it right for the sake of our children, and our nation.

NOTES

INTRODUCTION

1. www.hudexchange.info/resources/documents/2014-AHAR-Part1 .pdf, 22.

2. www.air.org/center/national-center-family-homelessness.

3. Kai Wright, "What Recovery?" *Harper's Magazine*, August 2015, 55.

4. Francis Walker, "The Causes of Poverty," *Century Magazine*, December 1897, 210–11.

5. Steve Liesman, www.cnbc.com/id/101524336.

CHAPTER I. NASHVILLE, TENNESSEE

1. Quoted in Robert Kelso, *The History of Public Poor Relief in Massachusetts* (Boston: Houghton Mifflin, 1922), 172.

2. Paula Poag, interview with author, December 2003.

3. Interview with author, April 2005.

4. www.colorado.edu/cye/sites/default/files/attached-files/outcasts .pdf, 4.

5. Ibid., 2.

6. Ellen Bassuk et al., "Post-Traumatic Stress Disorder in Extremely Poor Women: Implications for Health Care Clinicians," *Journal of the American Medical Women's Association* (Spring 2001), 79–85.

7. Ellen Bassuk et al., "The Characteristics and Needs of Sheltered Homeless and Low-Income Housed Mothers," *Journal of the American Medical Association* 276, no. 8 (August 28, 1996), 643.

8. Ellen Bassuk, interview with author, April 2009.

9. Bassuk, "Characteristics and Needs of Sheltered Homeless and Low-Income Housed Mothers," 645–47.

10. Patti Hassler, Children's Defense Fund, email, April 2015.

11. Robert Putnam, *Our Kids: The American Dream in Crisis* (New York: Simon & Schuster, 2015), 132.

12. Jennifer Cox, interview with author, December 2003.

13. Interview with author, December 2003.

14. William Bradford, *History of Plymouth Plantation,* book 2 (Boston, 1856), 9.

15. Francis Higginson, *New-England's Plantation with the Sea Journal and Other Writings,* (Salem, MA: Essex Book and Print Club, 1908), 118.

16. http://winthropsociety.com/doc_charity.php.

17. Walter Trattner, *From Poor Law to Welfare State* (New York: Free Press, 1994), 12–13.

18. Valerie Polakow, ed., *The Public Assault on America's Children* (New York: Teacher's College Press, 2000), 2.

19. Trattner, *From Poor Law to Welfare State,* 19.

20. Samuel Hayes Elliot, *New England's Chattels or Life in the Northern Poor-house.* (New York, H. Dayton, 1858), 35.

21. National Alliance to End Homelessness, www.endhomelessness.org/library/entry/rapid-re-housing-a-history-and-core-components.

22. National Alliance to End Homelessness, www.endhomelessness.org/page/-/files/Ending%20Family%20Homelessness%20Initiative%20final.pdf.

23. National Alliance to End Homelessness, www.endhomelessness.org/library/entry/rapid-re-housing-a-history-and-core-components.

24. Quoted in Josiah Henry Benton. *Warning Out in New England* (Boston: W. B. Clarke Co., 1911), 36.

25. Quoted in Robert Bremner, ed., *Children and Youth in America: A Documentary History, Vol. 1* (Cambridge, MA: Harvard University Press, 1970), 67.

26. Interview with author, April 2013.

27. Quoted in Bremner, *Children and Youth in America*, 38.

28. Ibid., 103.

29. www.cityofboston.gov/Images_Documents/Guide%20to%20the%20Almshouse%20records_tcm3–30021.pdf, 1.

30. Melanie McElhiney, interview with author, December 2007.

31. http://roomintheinn.org/sites/default/files/Spring2013News%20-%20less%20than%202MB.pdf, 5.

32. Joey Garrison, "Homeless Nonprofit Key Alliance in Disarray after Board Defections," *Nashville City Paper*, August 13, 2012, 6.

33. http://assets.thehcn.net/content/sites/ochca/10_Year_Plan_to_End_Homelessness_2012.pdf, 8.

34. www,nashville.gov/Social-Services/Homelessness-Commission/About-Homelessness/Homeless-Counts.aspx.

35. Will Connelly, interview with author, April 2013.

36. Kathryn J. Edin and H. Luke Shaefer, *$2.00 a Day: Living on Almost Nothing in America* (Boston: Houghton Mifflin Harcourt, 2015), 75.

37. Joyce Lavery, interview with author, April 2013.

38. Catherine Knowles, interview with author, April 2013.

39. Eric Hirsch, www.youtube.com/watch?v=3cQHi85Nm7s (2:40).

40. Elizabeth Fox, "Catherine Knowles: Faces of Nashville," http://styleblueprint.com/nashville/everyday/catherine-knowles-faces-nashville/.

41. Carolyn Grossley, interview with author, April 2013.

42. Interview with author, April 2013.

43. Eric Nellis and Anne Decker Cecere, eds., *The Eighteenth-Century Records of the Boston Overseers of the Poor* (Boston: Colonial Society of Massachusetts, 2007), 979.

CHAPTER 2. BOSTON, MASSACHUSETTS

1. Leslie Lawrence, telephone interview with author, January 2005.

2. www.tbf.org/~/media/TBFOrg/Files/Reports/2004%20Housing%20Report%20Card.pdf, 6.

3. Massachusetts Coalition for the Homeless, "The Road to Nowhere … Barriers Facing Families in Search of Shelter," http://files.eric.ed.gov/fulltext/ED466519.pdf, 15.

4. Jack Shonkoff, presentation at Horizons for Homeless Children National Conference, Cambridge, MA, May 20, 2013.

5. John C. Buckner, www.icphusa.org/index.asp?page=20&uncensored=9&story=61&pg=126, 1.

6. www.dshs.wa.gov/sites/default/files/SESA/rda/documents/research-11–203.pdf, 10.

7. Ibid., 5.

8. Mary Walsh, *Moving to Nowhere: Children's Stories of Homelessness* (Westport, CT: Auburn House, 1992), 110.

9. David Shipler, *The Working Poor* (New York: Knopf, Doubleday, 2008), 144–45.

10. Ellen Bassuk et al., "The Characteristics and Needs of Sheltered Homeless and Low-Income Housed Mothers," *Journal of the American Medical Association,* 276, no. 8 (August 28, 1996): 640–46.

11. Gary B. Nash, "Poverty and Politics," in *Down and Out in Early America,* ed. Billy G. Smith (University Park: Pennsylvania State University Press, 2004), 15.

12. Eric Nellis and Anne Decker Cecere, eds., *The Eighteenth-Century Records of the Boston Overseers of the Poor* (Boston: Colonial Society of Massachusetts, 2007), 64.

13. Billy G. Smith, "Poverty and Economic Marginality in Eighteenth Century America," *Proceedings of the American Philosophical Society* 132, no. 1 (March 1988), 101, 106.

14. Priscilla Ferguson Clement, *Welfare and the Poor in the Nineteenth-Century City* (Cranbury, NJ: Associated University Presses, 1985), 134.

15. Kelly Turley, interview with author, May 2013.

16. Quoted in Greg Shaw, *The Welfare Debate* (Westport CT: Greenwood Press, 2007), 26.

17. David Rothman, *The Discovery of the Asylum* (Boston: Little Brown, 1971), 163.

18. Quoted in ibid., 166.

19. Quoted in Homer Folks, *The Care of Destitute, Neglected, and Delinquent Children* (New York: Macmillan Co., 1907), 37.

20. Boston Almshouse Records, 1820, Massachusetts Historical Society, reel 11, box 12, folder 4.

21. Sanna J. Thompson and Makeba Pinder, www.sagepub.com /ritzerintro/study/materials/reference/77708_11.2ref.pdf, 4.

22. Nick Kourgialis et al., www.childrenshealthfund.org/sites /default/files/HFSNI-report.pdf, 16.

23. www.nhchc.org/resources/clinical/diseases-and-conditions /nutrition/.

24. Anonymous, *An Account of the Rise, Progress, and Present State of the Boston Female Asylum* (Boston: Russell and Cutler, 1803), 19.

25. Rothman, *Discovery of the Asylum,* 183.

26. Robert Bremner, *Children and Youth in America, Vol. 2, 1866–1932, Parts 1–6* (Cambridge, MA: Harvard University Press, 1971), 254.

27. Folks, *Care of Destitute, Neglected, and Delinquent Children,* 33–34.

28. David Wagner, *Ordinary People: In and out of Poverty in the Gilded Age* (Boulder, CO: Paradigm, 2008), 157.

29. Quoted in Ralph da Costa Nunez, *Hopes, Dreams, and Promise* (New York: Institute for Children and Poverty, 1994), 4.

30. John Wagner, interview with author, January 2005.

31. Leslie Lawrence, telephone interview with author, January 2005.

32. Kathleen Burge, "For Homeless Families, Hotel Is a Life in Limbo," *Boston Globe,* March 25, 2012, B-1.

33. Jenifer B. McKim, "Mass. to End Placing of Homeless in Motels," *Boston Globe,* January 2, 2013, Business.

34. Christopher Blagg et al., "Safe at Home: The Families of Home-BASE" (Boston: Metropolitan Boston Housing Partnership, May 2013), 14.

35. Ibid., 2.

36. Libby Hayes, interview with author, May 2013.

37. Interview with author, May 2013.

38. Libby Hayes, "Harsh State Regulations Leave Many Families out in the Cold," http://homesforfamilies.org/pdf/ProvidersPrinted.pdf.

39. www.mass.gov/hed/docs/dhcd/hs/hsn/hsn2016–01.pdf.

40. Jamie Minton, "Bringing It Home: Can a State Solve Homelessness? An Overview and Assessment of the Emergency Access Program," Brandeis University, Heller School for Social Policy and Management, May 2013, 13.

41. Ruth Bourquin and Liza Hirsch, "Out in the Cold: Homeless Children in Crisis in Massachusetts" (Boston: Massachusetts Law Reform Institute, April 2013), 1.

42. McKim, "Mass. to End Placing of Homeless in Motels."

43. Elizabeth Rogers, interview with author, July 2013.

44. http://children.massbudget.org/emergency-assistance-hotels-and-motels.

45. Steven A. Rosenberg, *Boston Globe*, November 16, 2014, www .bostonglobe.com/metro/regionals/north/2014/11/16/motels-becomes-kids-homes-danvers-waltham-weymouth/gIYha2mkhZY2cZaZoy3k1O /story.html.

46. Blagg et al., "Safe at Home," 14.

47. Michael W. Ames et al., "Massachusetts Economic Independence Index, 2013," Crittendon Women's Union, www.liveworkthrive .org/site/assets/docs/MASS%20INDEX%20FINALWEB.pdf, 1.

48. Interview with author, May 2013.

CHAPTER 3. FAIRFAX, VIRGINIA

1. Robert Hunter, *Poverty* (New York: Macmillan Co., 1904), 190–91.

2. Interview with author, May 2009.

3. Matthew Desmond, www.macfound.org/media/files/HHM _Research_Brief_-_Poor_Black_Women_Are_Evicted_at_Alarming _Rates.pdf, 1.

4. Anonymous, *The American Almanac of Family Homelessness* (New York: Institute for Children, Poverty, and Homelessness, 2013), 13.

5. Ibid.

6. Kaiser Foundation, "Poverty Rate by Race/Ethnicity, 2009," http://kff.org/other/state-indicator/poverty-rate-by-raceethnicity/.

7. Anonymous, *American Almanac of Family Homelessness*, 13.

8. http://forabettertexas.org/images/EO_2014_ACSPovertyIncome
_Charts.pdf, 11.

9. Anne M. Aviles, "Latinos, Immigrants, and Homelessness," in
Homelessness in America, ed. Robert Hartmann McNamara (Westport,
CT: Praeger, 2008), 205–6.

10. Neil L. Shumsky, *Homelessness: A Documentary and Reference Guide*
(Santa Barbara, CA: Greenwood, 2012), 329.

11. Billy G. Smith, "Poverty and Economic Marginality in Eighteenth-Century America," *Proceedings of the American Philosophical Society*
132, no. 1 (March 1988), 95.

12. Roger Daniels, *Coming to America: A History of Immigration and Ethnicity in American Life* (Princeton, NJ: Visual Education Corporation,
1990), 130.

13. Quoted in David Wagner, *Ordinary People: In and out of Poverty in
the Gilded Age* (Boulder, CO: Paradigm, 2008), 26–27.

14. Peter C. Holloran, *Boston's Wayward Children: Social Services for
Homeless Children, 1830–1930* (Boston: Northeastern University Press,
1994), 44.

15. Priscilla Ferguson Clement, *Growing Pains: Children in the Industrial Age, 1850–1890* (New York: Twayne, 1997), 16.

16. Daniels, *Coming to America,* 125–26.

17. Halloran, *Boston's Wayward Children,* 137.

18. Ferguson Clement, *Growing Pains,* 193–94.

19. Quoted in John E.B. Myers, *Child Protection in America:
Past, Present, and Future* (New York: Oxford University Press, 2006),
56–57.

20. Jordanna Packtor, www.borgenmagazine.com/4-worst-orphanages-
recent-history/.

21. Amy Sherman, www.politifact.com/florida/statements/2014/nov
/17/jack-seiler/jack-seiler-says-arnold-abbott-90-year-old-wasnt-t/.

22. http://nationalhomeless.org/wp-content/uploads/2014/10/Food-
Sharing2014.pdf?utm_source=Homelessness+in+the+News+10.14–10.20
.14&utm_campaign=Homelessness+in+the+News+9.30–10.6.14&utm_
medium=email.

23. Andrew L. Yarrow, file:///C:/Users/user/Downloads/Childrens-
Policy-History%20(1).pdf, 2.

24. Quoted in Robert Bremner, *Children and Youth in America, Vol. II, 1866–1932, Parts 1–6* (Cambridge, MA: Harvard University Press, 1971), 253–54.

25. Catherine Reef, *Alone in the World: Orphans and Orphanages in America* (New York: Clarion Books, 2005), 11.

26. Quoted in Robert Bremner, *American Philanthropy* Chicago: University of Chicago Press, 1988), 66.

27. Tycie Young, interview with author, May 2009.

28. Anonymous, *Second Annual Report of the Children's Aid Society* (New York: M. B. Wynkoop, 1855), 13–15.

29. David Nasaw, *Children of the City: At Work and at Play* (New York: Oxford University Press, 1985), 70.

30. www.childrensaidsociety.org/about/history/orphan-trains.

31. Quoted in www.kancoll.org/articles/orphans/or_news4.htm.

32. Quoted in Marilyn Irving Holt, *The Orphan Trains: Placing Out in America* (Lincoln: University of Nebraska Press, 1992), 116.

33. Charles Loring Brace, *The Dangerous Classes of New York and Twenty Years' Work among Them* (New York: Wynkoop and Hollenbeck, 1872), 224.

34. Kathi Sheffel, interview with author, May 2009.

35. Interview with author, May 2009.

36. Dean Klein, interview with author, May 2009.

37. Interview with author, May 2009.

38. www.fairfaxcounty.gov/homeless/point-in-time/pit-2014.htm.

39. Dean Klein, interview with author, May 2014.

40. Tom Jackman, "Fairfax County Reduced Homelessness by 16 Percent during Recession," *Washington Post,* June 20, 2011, 2-B.

41. Patrick Markee, interview with author, May 2014.

42. U.S. Department of Housing and Urban Development, "The 2013 Annual Assessment Report to Congress, www.hudexchange.info/resources/documents/ahar-2013-part1.pdf, 26.

43. Coalition for the Homeless, www.coalitionforthehomeless.org/wp-content/uploads/2014/04/State-of-the-Homeless-2014-FORMAT-TED-FINAL.pdf, 2.

44. Eric Durkin, "New York City Homeless Shelters See Record High Number of Children in 2014," www.nydailynews.com/news

/politics/exclusive-nyc-homeless-shelter-stays-kids-soar-article-1.2154843 ?cid = bitly.

45. Andrea Elliott and Rebecca R. Ruiz, "400 Children to Be Removed from 2 Shelters," *New York Times*, February 21, 2014, A-1.

46. www.hfhnyc.org.

47. "Rapidly Rehousing Homeless Families: New York City—A Case Study," policy opinion brief, Institute for Children, Poverty and Homelessness, April 2013, 5.

CHAPTER 4. PORTLAND, OREGON

1. *Proceedings of the Conference on the Care of Dependent Children* (Washington, DC: Government Printing Office, 1909), 7.

2. Anonymous, *BCC Pipeline*, September 1976, 2.

3. Kathleen Ryan and Mark Beach, *Burnside: A Community* (Portland, OR: Coast to Coast Books, 1979), 33.

4. Israel Bayer, interview with author, November 2014.

5. Figures provided by Portland Public Schools in email to author, October 23, 2014.

6. www.portlandoregon.gov/phb/article/513379, 5.

7. Annie Ellison, www.golocalpdx.com/news/portlands-rapid-economic-growth-leaves-poorest-oregonians-behind.

8. www.historyinink.com/909101%20T%20Roosevelt%20TLS.jpg.

9. Richard Archer, *Fissures in the Rock* (Hanover, NH: University Press of New England, 2001), 82.

10. http://pages.uoregon.edu/adoption/archive/Barrstats.htm.

11. www.childwelfare.gov/pubs/factsheets/foster.pdf#page=1&view =Key Findings, 3.

12. Troy Hammond, interview with author, November 2014.

13. Jean DeMaster, interview with author, November 2014.

14. Interview with author, November 2014.

15. Bobby Weinstock, "Affordable Rental Housing Crisis Hasn't Budged in Recovery," *Street Roots*, February 28, 2014, 11.

16. Interview with author, November 2014.

17. Tiffany Kingery, interview with author, October 2014.

18. Marti Heard, interview with author, October 2014.

19. Marc Jolin, interview with author, November 2014.

20. www.presidency.ucsb.edu/ws/?pid=22932.

21. Grace Abbott, *From Relief to Social Security: The Development of the New Public Welfare Service* (Washington, DC: Beard Books, 2001), 178.

22. www.monh.org/exhibitions/online-exhibitions/teenage-hoboes-in-the-great-depression/, section 3.

23. www.eyewitnesstohistory.com/snprelief1.htm.

24. Deborah Ward, *The White Welfare State: The Radicalization of U.S. Welfare Policy* (Ann Arbor: University of Michigan Press, 2005), 2.

25. www.ssa.gov/history/reports/ces/cesbookc13.html, 246.

26. Russell Freedman, *Children of the Great Depression* (New York: Houghton Mifflin Harcourt, 2010), 15.

27. National Association for the Education of Homeless Children and Youth, www.naehcy.org/educational-resources/youth.

28. Ibid.

29. www.endhomelessness.org/library/entry/an-emerging-framework-for-ending-unaccompanied-youth-homelessness.

30. Nicole Akoukou Thompson, www.latinpost.com/articles/15831/20140702/unaccompanied-and-undocumented-in-america-treatment-in-detention-centers-and-the-judicial-system.htm.

31. Errol Lincoln Uys, *Riding the Rails: Teenagers on the Move during the Great Depression* (New York: Routledge, 2003), 11.

32. Thomas Minehan, *Boy and Girl Tramps of America* (New York: Farrar & Rinehart, 1934), xiii.

33. Uys, *Riding the Rails,* 32.

34. www.socialwelfarehistory.com/programs/aid-to-dependent-children-the-legal-history/.

35. www.washingtonpost.com/blogs/wonkblog/wp/2013/09/23/why-are-47-million-americans-on-food-stamps-its-the-recession-mostly/.

36. http://febp.newamerica.net/background-analysis/head-start.

37. www.theotx.org/wp-content/uploads/2014/09/HeadStart_Reauthorization.pdf.

38. Kathryn J. Edin and H. Luke Shaefer, *$2.00 a Day: Living on Almost Nothing in America* (Boston: Houghton Mifflin Harcourt, 2015), 7–8.

39. Ian Frazier, www.newyorker.com/magazine/2013/10/28.

40. Ellen L. Bassuk and William R. Beardslee, "Depression in Homeless Mothers: Addressing an Unrecognized Public Health Issue," *American Journal Orthopsychiatry* 84, no. 1 (2014), 73.

41. Valerie Polakow, *Hard Lives, Mean Streets* (Boston: Northeastern University Press, 2010), 2–3.

42. Sabrina Tavernise, "Project to Improve Poor Children's Intellect Led to Better Health," *New York Times,* March 28, 2014, A-16.

CHAPTER 5. TRENTON, NEW JERSEY

1. Robert Putnam, *Our Kids: The American Dream in Crisis* (New York: Simon & Schuster, 2015), 261.

2. Althea Arnold et al., "Out of Reach 2014," http://nlihc.org /oor/2014.

3. Judith A. Dulberger, *"Mother Donit fore the Best"* (Syracuse, NY: Syracuse University Press, 1996), 10.

4. Virginia Young, www.stltoday.com/news/local/govt-and-politics /missouri-legislature-enacts-limit-on-welfare-benefits-over-nixon-s /article_22e44a54-b286–50e5–8236-fdaf93c1b2e3.html.

5. Rudy Takala, http://news.heartland.org/newspaper- article/2015 /02/25/missouri-senate-passes-welfare-reform-bill.

6. www.neighborhoodscout.com/nj/trenton/crime/.

7. Nancy Phillips, http://articles.philly.com/1987 11–22/news/26174431 _1_permanent-housing-homeless-people-housing-policy.

8. www.merceralliance.org.

9. http://b.3cdn.net/naeh/880fb35b6224742820_x4m6id5cn.pdf, 5.

10. Marygrace Billek, interview with author, May 2014.

11. Connie Mercer, interview with author, June 2014.

12. Interview with author, June 2014.

CONCLUSION

1. Robert Hunter, *Poverty* (New York: Macmillan Co., 1905), 235.

2. Michael B. Katz, *In the Shadow of the Poorhouse: A Social History of Welfare in America* (New York: Basic Books, 1996), 41–42.

3. Dwight MacDonald, www.newyorker.com/archive/1963/01/19 /1963_01_19_082_TNY_CARDS_000075671#ixzz26upkbwkw.

4. www.endhomelessness.org/pages/national_housing_trust_fund.

5. Norbert J. Michel and John L. Ligon, www.heritage.org/research /reports/2013/11/gse-reform-affordable-housing-trust-funds-or-slush-funds.

6. Ibid.

7. Shiv Rawal, http://thinkprogress.org/economy/2015/05/04/3654419 /national-housing-trust-fund-republicans/.

8. National Alliance to End Homelessness, www.endhomelessness .org/library/entry/rapid-re-housing-a-history-and-core-components.

ACKNOWLEDGMENTS

First and foremost, thanks go to Anne Paine who sheltered me for long periods of time in Nashville, and without whose kindness and generosity this book might not have been written.

And many thanks to the other people who encouraged me while I did my research. In Nashville, the late John Egerton, the LeQuire family (Alan, Andrée, and Acadia), Warren Duzak, and Clare Bratten; in the Boston area, Sue Katz and Steve Yarbrough; in Portland, Chris Ryan, Cacilda Jethá, Susan Emmons, Bobby Weinstock, the Gies family (Martha, Julia, and Michael), and Jim Jordan; in Fairfax, Nancy Hartzenbusch and Luisa D'Arista.

My love and thanks for their support go to my family, including sister-in-law Jean Schweid, my late, sorely missed brother David, my nephews Ben and Doug, my son Daniel Winunwe Rivers and his partner Jessica Delgado, and most especially to my wife and companion, Carmen Martínez Gómez.

Thanks also to Elaine Maisner whose input was a great help.

And to keep it short, a deep bow of gratitude to all those people interviewed herein who cared enough to sit down and talk with me, and to all the people at the University of California Press who helped bring this book to fruition.

As always, responsibility for errors is mine alone.

BIBLIOGRAPHY

Abramsky, Sasha. *The American Way of Poverty: How the Other Half Still Lives*. New York: Nation Books, 2013.

Anonymous. *An Account of the Rise, Progress, and Present State of the Boston Female Asylum*. Boston: Russell and Cutler, 1803.

———. *Second Annual Report of the Children's Aid Society*. New York: M.B. Wynkoop, 1855.

———. *The Almshouse Experience: Collected Reports*. New York: Arno Press, 1971.

———. *Annual Reports of the Children's Aid Society: Nos. 1–10, Feb. 1854–Feb. 1863*. New York: Arno Press and New York Times, 1971.

———. *The American Almanac of Family Homelessness*. New York: Institute for Children, Poverty, and Homelessness, 2013.

Archer, Richard. *Fissures in the Rock*. Hanover, NH: University Press of New England, 2001.

Arrighi, Barbara A. *America's Shame: Women and Children in Shelter and the Degradation of Family Roles*. Westport, CT: Praeger, 1997.

Ashby, LeRoy. *Saving the Waifs*. Philadelphia: Temple University Press, 1984.

Barak, Gregg. *Gimme Shelter: A Social History of Homelessness in Contemporary America*. Westport, CT: Praeger, 1991.

Barrows, Israel, ed. *Proceedings of the National Conference of Charities and Correction, 1884.* Boston: George H. Ellis, 1885.

Baumohl, Jim, ed. *Homelessness in America.* Phoenix, AZ: Oryx Press, 1996.

Benton, Josiah Henry. *Warning Out in New England.* Boston: W. B. Clarke Co., 1911.

Brace, Charles Loring. *The Dangerous Classes of New York and Twenty Years' Work among Them.* New York: Wynkoop and Hollenbeck, 1872.

Bradford, William. *History of Plymouth Plantation, Book 2.* Boston, 1856.

Bremner, Robert. *From the Depths.* New York: New York University Press, 1956.

⸻, ed. *Children and Youth in America: A Documentary History, Vol. 1.* Cambridge, MA: Harvard University Press, 1970.

⸻. *Children and Youth in America, Vol. 2, 1866–1932, Parts 1–6.* Cambridge, MA: Harvard University Press, 1971.

⸻. *American Philanthropy.* Chicago: University of Chicago Press, 1988.

Bridenbaugh, Carl. *Cities in the Wilderness: The First Century of Urban Life in America.* New York: Oxford University Press, 1971.

Broder, Sherri. *Tramps, Unfit Mothers and Neglected Children.* Philadelphia: University of Pennsylvania Press, 2002.

Bulman, Philip. *Caught in the Mix: An Oral Portrait of Homelessness.* Westport, CT: Praeger, 1993.

Calhoun, Arthur W. *Social History of the American Family, Vol. 1.* Cleveland: Arthur Clark Co., 1917.

Caton, Carol. *Homeless in America.* New York: Oxford University Press, 1990.

Choi, Namkee G., and Lidia J. Snyder. *Homeless Families with Children: A Subjective Experience of Homelessness.* New York: Springer, 1999.

Cone, T. E. *History of American Pediatrics.* Boston: Little Brown, 1979.

da Costa Nunez, Ralph. *Hopes, Dreams, and Promise.* New York: Institute for Children and Poverty, 1994.

⸻. *The New Poverty: Homeless Families in America.* New York: Plenum Press, 1994.

————. *Beyond the Shelter Wall: Homeless Families Speak Out.* New York: White Tiger Press, 2004.

————. *A Shelter Is Not a Home ... Or Is It? Family Homelessness in New York City.* New York: Institute for Children and Poverty, 2010.

da Costa Nunez, Ralph, and Ethan G. Sribnick. *The Poor among Us.* New York: White Tiger Press, 2013.

Daniels, Roger. *Coming to America: A History of Immigration and Ethnicity in American Life.* Princeton, NJ: Visual Education, 1990.

DeParle, Jason. *American Dream: Three Women, Ten Kids, and a Nation's Drive to End Welfare.* New York: Viking Penguin, 2004.

DePastino, Todd. *Citizen Hobo: How a Century of Homelessness Shaped America.* Chicago: University of Chicago Press, 2005.

Desmond, Matthew. *Evicted: Poverty and Profit in the American City.* New York: Crown, 2016.

Dulberger, Judith A. *"Mother Donit fore the Best."* Syracuse, NY: Syracuse University Press, 1996.

Earle, Alice Morse. *Child Life in Colonial Days.* New York: Macmillan Co., 1899.

Edelman, Peter. *So Rich, So Poor: Why It's So Hard to End Poverty in America.* New York: New Press, 2012.

Edin, Kathryn J., and H. Luke Shaefer. *$2.00 a Day: Living on Almost Nothing in America.* Boston: Houghton Mifflin Harcourt, 2015.

Elliot, Samuel Hayes. *New England's Chattels or Life in the Northern Poorhouse.* New York: H. Dayton, 1858.

Ferguson Clement, Priscilla. *Welfare and the Poor in the Nineteenth-Century City.* Cranbury, NJ: Associated University Presses, 1985.

————. *Growing Pains: Children in the Industrial Age, 1850–1890.* New York: Twayne, 1997.

Field, Edward, ed. *State of Rhode Island and Providence Plantations at the End of the Century: A History, Vol. 3.* Boston: Mason Publishing Company, 1902.

Folks, Homer. *The Care of Destitute, Neglected, and Delinquent Children.* New York: Macmillan Co., 1907.

Freedman, Russell. *Children of the Great Depression.* New York: Houghton Mifflin Harcourt, 2010.

Friedman, Donna Haig. *Parenting in Public: Family Shelter and Public Assistance.* New York: Columbia University Press, 2000.

Golden, Stephanie. *The Meanings and Myths of Homelessness.* Berkeley: University of California Press, 1993.

Gordon, Linda. *Heroes of Their Own Lives: The Politics and History of Family Violence—Boston, 1880–1960.* Champaign: University of Illinois Press, 2002.

Hacsi, Timothy. *Second Home: Orphan Asylums and Poor Families in America.* Cambridge, MA: Harvard University Press, 1997.

Haskins, George Lee. *Law and Authority in Early Massachusetts.* New York: Macmillan, 1960.

Hawes, Joseph M. *Children in Urban Society: Juvenile Delinquency in Nineteenth-Century America.* New York: Oxford University Press, 1971.

Hawke, David Freeman. *Everyday Life in Early America.* New York: Harper & Row, 1988.

Herndon, Ruth Wallis. *Unwelcome Americans: Living on the Margin in Early New England.* Philadelphia: University of Pennsylvania Press, 2001.

Holloran, Peter C. *Boston's Wayward Children: Social Services for Homeless Children, 1830–1930.* Boston: Northeastern University Press, 1994.

Higginson, Francis. *New-England's Plantation with the Sea Journal and Other Writings.* Salem, MA: Essex Book and Print Club, 1908.

Hunter, Robert. *Poverty.* New York: Macmillan Co., 1905.

Irving Holt, Marilyn. *The Orphan Trains: Placing Out in America.* Lincoln: University of Nebraska Press, 1992.

Jackson, Karleen. *Family Homelessness: More than Simply a Lack of Housing.* New York: Garland, 2000.

Katz, Michael B. *In the Shadow of the Poorhouse: A Social History of Welfare in America.* New York: Basic Books, 1996.

Katzman, David M. *Plain Folk.* Urbana: University of Illinois Press, 1982.

Kelso, Robert. *The History of Public Poor Relief in Massachusetts* Boston: Houghton Mifflin, 1922.

Keppler, Patricia Manning. *Poor Relief in Massachusetts Bay: Seventeenth Century Boston.* Master's thesis, Northeastern University, 1973.

Komisar, Lucy. *Down and Out in the USA: A History of Social Welfare.* London: Franklin Watts, 1973.

Kozol, Jonathan. *Rachel and Her Children: Homeless Families in America.* New York: Crown, 1988.

Kusmer, Kenneth L. *Down and Out on the Road: The Homeless in American History.* New York: Oxford University Press, 2002.

Kyle, Ken. *Contextualizing Homelessness.* New York: Routledge, 2005.

Langsam, Miriam Z. *Children West: A History of the Placing-out of the New York Children's Aid Society, 1853–1890.* Master's thesis, University of Wisconsin, Madison, 1964.

Levinson, David. *Encyclopedia of Homelessness.* Thousand Oaks, CA: Sage, 2004.

Lindsey, Duncan. *The Welfare of Children.* New York: Oxford University Press, 1994.

Marten, James, ed. *Children in Colonial America.* New York: New York University Press, 2007.

McNamara, Robert Hartmann, ed. *Homelessness in America.* Westport, CT: Praeger, 2008.

Minehan, Thomas. *Boy and Girl Tramps of America.* New York: Farrar & Rinehart, 1934.

Mingione, Enzo, ed. *Urban Poverty and the Underclass.* Cambridge, MA: Wiley Blackwell, 1996.

Morgan, E. S. *The Puritan Family.* Boston: Trustees of the Public Library, 1944.

Myers, John E.B. *Child Protection in America: Past, Present, and Future.* New York: Oxford University Press, 2006.

Nasaw, David. *Children of the City: At Work and at Play.* New York: Oxford University Press, 1985.

Nellis, Eric, and Anne Decker Cecere, eds. *The Eighteenth-Century Records of the Boston Overseers of the Poor.* Boston: Colonial Society of Massachusetts, 2007.

Nevins, Allen, and Milton Halsey Thomas, eds. *The Diary of George Templeton Strong: The Turbulent Fifties, 1850–1859.* New York: Macmillan, 1952.

Polakow, Valerie, ed. *The Public Assault on America's Children.* New York: Teacher's College Press, 2000.

———, ed. *Hard Lives, Mean Streets.* Boston: Northeastern University Press, 2010.

Putnam, Robert. *Our Kids: The American Dream in Crisis.* New York: Simon & Schuster, 2015.

Reef, Catherine. *Alone in the World: Orphans and Orphanages in America.* New York: Clarion Books, 2005.

Riis, Jacob. *How the Other Half Lives: Studies among the Tenements of New York.* New York: Charles Scribner's Sons, 1890.

———. *The Children of the Poor.* New York: Charles Scribner's Sons, 1908.

Rochefort, David A. *From Poorhouses to Homelessness: Policy Analysis and Mental Health Care.* Westport, CT: Auburn House, 1993.

Romasco, Albert U. *The Poverty of Abundance.* London: Oxford University Press, 1965.

Rothman, David J. *The Discovery of the Asylum.* Boston: Little Brown, 1971.

———, ed. *The Jacksonians on the Poor: Collected Pamphlets.* New York: Arno Press, 1971.

Ruttman, Darrett B. *Winthrop's Boston: A Portrait of a Puritan Town, 1630–1649.* Chapel Hill: University of North Carolina Press, 1965.

Ruttman, Darrett B., and Anita H. Ruttman. *A Place in Time: Middlesex County, Virginia, 1650–1750.* New York: Norton, 1984.

Ryan, Kathleen, and Mark Beach. *Burnside: A Community.* Portland, OR: Coast to Coast Books, 1979.

Schouler, James. *Americans of 1776.* New York: Dodd, Mead & Co., 1906.

Shaw, Greg. *The Welfare Debate.* Westport, CT: Greenwood Press, 2007.

Shipler, David. *The Working Poor.* New York: Knopf, Doubleday, 2008.

Shumsky, Neil L. *Homelessness: A Documentary and Reference Guide.* Santa Barbara, CA: Greenwood, 2012.

Smith, Billy G., ed. *Down and Out in Early America.* University Park: Pennsylvania State University Press, 2004.

Stansell, Christine. *City of Women: Sex and Class in New York 1789–1860.* Urbana: University of Illinois Press, 1987.

Trattner, Walter. *From Poor Law to Welfare State.* New York: Free Press, 1994.

Uys, Errol Lincoln. *Riding the Rails: Teenagers on the Move during the Great Depression*. New York: Routledge, 2003.

Van der Zee, John. *Bound Over*. New York: Simon & Schuster, 1985.

Vissing, Yvonne Marie. *Out of Sight, out of Mind: Homeless Children and Families in Small-town America*. Lexington: University Press of Kentucky, 1996.

Wagner, David. *The Poorhouse: America's Forgotten Institution*. Lanham, MD: Rowman & Littlefield, 2005.

———. *Ordinary People: In and out of Poverty in the Gilded Age*. Boulder, CO: Paradigm, 2008.

Walsh, Mary. *Moving to Nowhere: Children's Stories of Homelessness*. Westport, CT: Auburn House, 1992.

Wendinger, Renee. *Extra! Extra! The Orphan Trains and Newsboys of New York*. Sleepy Eye, MN: Legendary, 2009.

Williams, Jane Calterone. *A Roof over My Head: Women and the Shelter Industry*. Boulder, CO: University Press of Colorado, 2003.

INDEX

Abbott, Arnold, 106
Abouela, Talia, 121–124, 132
Addison, Sheila, 176
Aid to Families with Dependent
  Children (AFDC), 22,160–161,
  162
Albany Orphan Asylum, 169
Alger, Horatio Jr., 111
Almshouses, 67–68, 108, 139,164;
  and New York's Children's Law,
  107; deaths in Boston Alms-
  house, 69; during Civil War, 102;
  first in Boston, 31; functioning
  of, 31–32; nutrition in, 70–71;
  population of Boston alms-
  house, 64; regulations for
  Boston almshouse, 48–49; in
  Massachusetts, 72–73; resur-
  gence in twenty-first century,
  178–179
American Recovery and Reinvestment Act (ARRA), 173
Anchorage Motel, 91–94, 120; and
  FACETS, 122, 132; and Tiffany
Wilson, 117–118; as schoolbus
  stop, 121; distance from
  Laundromat, 95; meal distribution at, 105, 122
Apprenticeship, 27, 73, 101, 140; and
  age; 31; contracts for, 30; in
  Industrial Age, 68

Badges: worn by poor, 63
Bassuk, Ellen, 12–15, 62, 164
Bayer, Israel, 136–137
BCC Pipeline, 135, 136
Bill for the Benefit of the Indigent
  Insane, 108
Billek, Marygrace, 173–174, 177
Blake, Sandra, 47–49
Bloomberg, Michael, 129
Boarding out, 23, 25, 112
Bookmobile, 6
Boston Children's Mission,
  101–102
Brace, Charles Loring, 110, 112, 114
Bradford, William, 20
Brown, Isaiah, 27–28, 36, 42

Grossley, Carolyn, 45–47
Gupta, Deepak, 18–19, 33, 34

Hammond, Troy, 141
Harrington, Michael, 182–183
Harris, Clifton, 38, 39
Hart, Hastings, 104
Hawthorne Bridge, 155
Hayes, Libby, 80, 82, 86
Head Start program, 161–162
Heard, Marti, 137, 152
Heartlander Magazine, 170
Heckman, James, 166
Heller School for Social Policy
    and Management, 83
Heritage Foundation, 184
Higginson, Francis, 20–21
Hinojosa, Maria, 159
Hobo News, 135
HomeBase, 79–82, 83, 85
HomeFront, 174–175, 176, 177
Homeless children: and toxic
    stress, 165; asthma among, 69;
    health of, 11–12; numbers of, xv;
    nutrition of, 69; risk of abuse, 12;
    separate housing of, 73
Homeless families, 183; African
    American and Latino percent-
    ages, 97–99; depression among
    mothers, 164; eliminating family
    homelessness, 170, 183, 185;
    failure to eradicate family
    homelessness, 181; half main-
    tained by single mothers, 165;
    homeless grandparents caring
    for grandchildren, 16–17;
    national numbers, xv, xvi;
    numbers in Portland, 137
Homeless Prevention and Rapid
    Rehousing Program, 119
Homelessness: and Massachusetts
    colony, 19–27, 29; and Post-

traumatic Stress Disorder, 14;
    and violence, 14; changing
    demographic of, xiv; criminal-
    ization of, 105–106; federal
    policy toward, 108
Homes for Families, 79, 82;
Homes for the Homeless (HFH),
    131
Hoover, Herbert, 156, 169, 183;
    Hoovervilles, 157
Housing and Economic Recovery
    Act, 183
Housing first, 132; and Fairfax
    County, 126; and Mercer
    County, 172; as best practice,
    120; as outdoor relief, 24;
    opposition to, 130. *See also* Rapid
    rehousing
Housing locator network, 127
Housing readiness, 40; and New
    York City, 130; and transitional
    housing, 178; compared to rapid
    rehousing, 143
Human Solutions, 141–143, 152, 153
Hunter, Robert, 90, 180

Immigration, 65; contemporary,
    97–99; nineteenth century,
    99–103. *See also* Homeless
    Families
Indenture, 139, 140; contracts for,
    30; from almshouses, 31, 71; in
    "Individual" and "structural"
    explanations of poverty, xvii
Industrial Age 68, 101
Indoor relief, 167, 178; and emer-
    gency shelters 169; as punitive,
    49; spread of, 31; 63
Industrial Age, 68, 99, 113
Inhabitancy, 26–27
Institute for Children, Poverty
    and Homelessness (ICPH), 131

Intemperance: among the poor, 63, 67
Interstate Commerce Commission, 160

James Mott Community Assistance, 95–96
Jamestown, xiii
Jefferson, Cheryl, 175–176
Johnson, Lyndon, 161, 162, 182–183
JOIN, 152–153.
Jolin, Marc, 152–153
Journal of the American Medical Association (JAMA), 15, 61

Katz, Michael, 181
Kertman, Matt, 145
King, Martin Luther, Jr., 167
Kingery, Tiffany, 151
Klein, Dean, 118–120, 124–127
Knowles, Catherine, 33, 43–45

Lavery, Joyce, 42–43
Lawrence, Leslie, 76
Lee Highway, 95
López, Rodrigo, 148–151

MacDonald, Dwight, 182
MacDonald, Jim, 96
Markee, Patrick, 127–130
Massachusetts Board of State Charities, 72
Massachusetts Coalition for the Homeless (MCH), 54, 57, 66, 76
Massachusetts Department of Housing and Community Development (DHCD), 79, 84, 85
Massachusetts Department of Transitional Assistance (DTA), 54, 76, 79; commissioner of,

74–75; eligibility requirements, 57; referrals, 56; spending on emergency shelter, 75
Massachusetts Law Reform Institute, 83
Mayflower, xiii, 19–20, 139
McElhiney, Melanie, 33, 34, 44
McKinney-Vento Act, 7, 16,115
Medicare, 161
Medicaid, 161
Mercer Alliance to End Homelessness, 172, 177
Mercer County, New Jersey, 170–173, 176, 178
Mercer, Connie, 174–175, 176–177
Merrill, Fannie, 101
Merrill, George, 101–102, 110
Metropolitan Homeless Commission (Nashville), 38–42
Minehan, Thomas, 159
Mobile housing specialist: in Portland, 141, 143, 147, 151, 153
Money management classes, 40, 109, 144
Mother's pension, 157
Multnomah County, and rental assistance, 151; and winter shelter 141; homeless family system of care, 151

Nash, Gary, 63
National Alliance to End Homelessness (NAEH), 24, 120; evaluating Fairfax County, 125–126; evaluating Mercer County, 172, 173
National Association for the Education of Homeless Children and Youth, 158